Empowering Young Children

This essential guidebook offers creative, exciting ways for teachers to implement and support deep, authentic and transformative learning in early childhood. Each standalone chapter identifies a key focus for empowering children, exploring the research behind the habit, how it stimulates deep learning and the ways in which it can help address implicit hierarchies and disrupt oppression. Chapters feature hands-on activities, ideas for lessons and events that teachers can try, alongside techniques to involve parents and families, bringing this important work beyond the classroom walls.

Wendy L. Ostroff is an applied developmental and cognitive psychologist, and Professor in the Hutchins School of Liberal Studies at Sonoma State University, USA.

Empowering Young Children

How to Nourish Deep, Transformative Learning For Social Justice

Wendy L. Ostroff

Routledge
Taylor & Francis Group

NEW YORK AND LONDON

Cover image: © Getty Images

First published 2023
by Routledge
605 Third Avenue, New York, NY 10158

and by Routledge
4 Park Square, Milton Park, Abingdon, Oxon, OX14 4RN

Routledge is an imprint of the Taylor & Francis Group, an informa business

© 2023 Wendy L. Ostroff

Library of Congress Cataloging-in-Publication Data
A catalog record for this title has been requested

ISBN: 978-1-032-06575-5 (hbk)
ISBN: 978-1-032-06506-9 (pbk)
ISBN: 978-1-003-20287-5 (ebk)

DOI: 10.4324/9781003202875

Typeset in Palatino
by Newgen Publishing UK

This book is dedicated to the dearest, most dedicated of Dads:

David Ostroff

For a lifetime of loving generosities, large and small

And for all he undertook for the Cooks Brook Book Nook

Contents

Acknowledgments

I am grateful to have been given the opportunity to write this book, which has been percolating in my mind for many years – maybe even since I was a small child myself, wishing to do big things. I am grateful to Misha Kydd at Routledge for reaching out to me and believing in me and supporting a very different project than initially proposed: the project in my heart. Thank you to the reviewers who so enthusiastically responded to the idea, and thank you to Olivia Powers, Priyanka Mundada and Makenzi Crouch for bringing it to reality.

A huge thank you to my dear friend Heidi Saleh for encouraging me to say yes; also, for just being her hardcore, inspirational self and for offering myriad gracious and concrete support along the way! Thank you also to the friends of my mind who helped me gather the initial themes and find words to hold them: Estelle Broyer for empathy, Bob Brocken for being, Cécile LePage for nourishment, Jamie S. Cooper for attunement and Eric Common for "Rethinking Learning."

Immense thanks always to every one of my colleagues at the Hutchins School of Liberal Studies at Sonoma State University, past and present, for questioning systems of power and education; for decades of trust and autonomy. And thank you to my wonderfully game students, who bring such courage and talent to the seminar table, who have had a hard couple of years and yet have retained energy and hope for social justice work with children. Thank you to the stewards of the Sonoma State University RSCAP program for the gift of time.

I am overflowing with gratitude for those who helped me germinate and grow this book by sharing their philosophies and stories and gifts and enthusiasms. Mallory Muniz, Mutombo M'Panya, Buzz Kellogg, Megan McIlreavy, Ben Frymer, Geordie Lynch, Roland Vallet, Rachel Treat, Peter Kalill, Kurt Stanco and

Kate Dillon all graciously contributed. Thank you so much to Julie Mountcastle, Jennifer Staple Clark and the Slate School Education Idea Lab for igniting and sustaining such profound dialogues and connections. And thank you to those role models in my life, like Ernest Bromley, Robin Panneton and Tony Mountain, from whom I have learned so much about empowerment and justice, teaching, writing and thinking.

I am so indebted to my lovely friend Marisol DiNardo, my first reader – for her incisive suggestions, and for helping me find my voice through our many conversations. That this book was developed and birthed alongside hers (with both ultimately being about openness to possibilities) is in no small part due to the inspiration of "our girl." A heartfelt thank you to Margaret Anderson for her unequivocal depth, intuition and articulation; for the kind of perception and conjuring that only comes from inhabiting the WM Realm. And for the hours. Always the hours. Much gratitude to Cécile LePage, for introducing me to unique writers and pedagogues, and for engaging so deeply and insightfully in our many exchanges over the years, which have never failed to help me see things differently (and with more complexity). And a very special thank you to James H. McMahon, Jr., the original divergent thinker, for his pure-hearted and generous presence, and for teaching me about chemistry and lightness, all those years ago and still.

It is hard to imagine garnering the privilege to write without the support of my family. Thank you from the bottom of my heart to David and Susanne Ostroff, and Carmen and Carol Genova. And thank you to Jane Ostroff Lin, for her empowered energy and unique brilliance. Thank you to Sonia Genova, my joyful and creative muse, for the Koob Bulc and the Ladies Auxiliary; for serious silliness and precise awareness of all kinds. Thank you to Alexei Genova, philosopher and questioner of social facts extraordinaire, for thinking deeply and schooling me in so many things (not least, how to find and replace underscores!) Thank you to Shelldon, for balancing all of us out with a chill and easygoing style. And deepest, unending thanks to Rob Genova, for supporting and championing me and this project every step of the way – with so many conversations, so many ideas! For building the space! Picking up the slack! For being a quintessential, open-minded experimenter of the highest order!

Finally, utmost gratitude to my wise council of angels: Eleanor Louise Ostroff, Fay Afaf Kanafani and Heidi Jeanne Ostroff – who inspire and guide me daily (hourly!) from the undying lands. I love you all so much.

About the Author

Wendy L. Ostroff, Ph.D., is an applied developmental and cognitive psychologist, and Professor in the Hutchins School of Liberal Studies at Sonoma State University, a pioneering interdisciplinary and seminar-based program that prepares prospective teacher-learners to be critical readers, writers and thinkers who bridge cognitive science with innovative pedagogies. The author of two previous books, *Understanding How Young Children Learn* (2012) and *Cultivating Curiosity in K–12 Classrooms* (2016), and numerous articles, Dr. Ostroff is an award-winning educator with more than 20 years of experience in state-of-the-art teacher training. She leads workshops and professional development events worldwide on curiosity, cognition and the brain. www.wendyostroff.com

Introduction to *Empowering Young Children*

Young children are bursting with joyful and unstoppable urges: to play and move, to connect and communicate, to notice and explore. Their brains and minds are uniquely set up to learn, having evolved to do so over tens of thousands of years. Children are the greatest learners, as a matter of fact – far more adept than adults at gaining some of the most complex cognitive skills, like learning languages, using evidence to determine causal patterns and playing musical instruments (Gopnik, Griffiths & Lucas, 2015; Snow & Hoefnagel-Höhle, 1978; White-Schwoch, Woodruff Carr, Anderson, Strait & Kraus, 2013). As early childhood educators, we can harness children's natural gifts and proclivities and make them the foundation of our teaching. When we teach kids in the way they are set up to learn, they learn more readily and they learn things for longer. Decades of research in the learning sciences has shown that empowering young children sets them up for all of the virtues we dream of for them – empathy, self-determination, engagement, innovation, patience, embodied presence, perspective taking and comfort with discomfort. These dispositions are the foundation of just and equitable communities; they are at the heart of democratic engagement and in the minds of wise, thoughtful people.

DOI: 10.4324/9781003202875-1

Children are ideally positioned to develop into citizens who take responsibility for themselves and others in a socially just manner. This is because kids care deeply about fairness and friendship, similarities and differences; they are also unstoppable questioners of oft taken for granted assumptions and frameworks. When children develop their own perspectives, ideas and voices, they become better able to act and speak out against inequity and injustice in the classroom and in the wider community. When we put our best energy into nourishing children as unique and interesting humans, we can start to believe that the disparities of power throughout history can be changed and that we can contribute to that change.

There is an abundance of compelling empirical evidence for the benefits of teaching to empower children, from the fields of cognitive and developmental science, neuroscience, anthropology and sociology. The purpose of this book is to compile this evidence and to support teachers by providing them with a creative and exciting framework for implementing deep, authentic and transformative learning on the ground. When we work with how kids already *are*, rather than trying to tame them and make them suit us – we discover that their gifts are ideally situated for both transformative learning and social justice.

Respecting Children's Unique Perspectives

Kids' inner workings, desires, thoughts and ideas are just as worthy as those of adults'. They experience life in distinct and unusual ways, making them powerful teachers and philosophers. However, most children have very little control over their time, their thoughts or their behaviors. Often, because they still need care and guidance, children's voices and opinions are discounted from meaningful deliberation and decision-making. Children are not merely unformed adults; they are human beings in their own right. And yet, children are routinely disenfranchised in their homes and in their schools. More and more, kids' lives are structured, scheduled up and bossed around by adults all day, every day.

Suppose instead that we listened to and respected children's perspectives and held their questions in high regard. What if we let kids decide how to spend their own time, or trusted their intuitive responses? What if we empowered children to learn and grow the way they have naturally evolved and developed, without imposing our agendas on them? What if we let them choose how to fully spend one school day a week, or one day a month? Suppose they did choose to spend that whole day at recess, or to finally experiment with the science and math materials the way they wanted to? What if their school curriculum was focused on exploring and explaining those things that kids were wildly interested in?

Challenging Social Facts

Empowering children means taking their perspectives – listening to them and checking our own biases. It also may require a rethinking of our systems of education, which are rarely set up from the child's perspective. Granted, top-down structure can and does make everything easier for those in power; it makes learning appear linear and visible and sets up an accountability structure for teachers. The trouble is, the best learning is rarely linear or visible. We need to reassess what we're up to when we see, for instance, well-meaning teachers disrupting kids that are in a flow state at recess (perhaps adding and subtracting rocks from a puddle), in order to transition them inside to math class, to complete, say, an addition and subtraction worksheet. Instances like this are commonplace in schools when rigid schedules and top-down directions rule the day. This has created a significant mismatch between how young children best learn and how schools typically operate.

Here is a question to illustrate this mismatch: did you study a foreign language in school? Do you speak that language fluently today? If you were lucky enough to grow up in a country that starts second language instruction in early childhood, you very well might. But if you grew up in a country that begins second language instruction in middle or high school (like most schools in the U.S.) and did not ever live in a place that speaks the language you studied, I can predict with close to 100% certainty that you do not. Decades of cognitive science and neuroscience research has shown that children's brains are staggeringly adept at learning languages when they are young, but this learning has a critical period (defined by closing off synapses and eliminating myelination). By puberty, it becomes exponentially harder to learn a second language (and close to impossible to learn to speak it as a native speaker would) (Lee, Meltzoff, & Kuhl 2020). Yet, most schools in the U.S. begin teaching second languages in middle or high school, *at the exact moment when it becomes impossible to learn*, rendering all of that instruction useless. Why would we set up schools that way? These choices may be made out of tradition or convenience. But often they are based on social facts that haven't been questioned in a long time, if ever. And the folks who best understand how children learn (who sit upon mountains of systematic, solid research such as this) almost never talk to the folks who decide on the mandated curriculum for kids. They don't talk to each other because they don't even know each other. It's as if they don't even speak the same language.

The ways that we raise and educate our children are beset with unexamined assumptions that need to be revisited and challenged. French sociologist Emile Durkheim called mechanisms that control us (which we are largely unaware of) "social facts" (Durkheim, 1938). This book asks us to question the social facts about kids and learning and school and society. We must shake up our version of what *has to be* in educational contexts, and to do that, we must reconsider all of the social facts about the children in our midst. But in order to challenge the social facts, first we need to notice them – this will take close attention in addition to bravery. Every time we are faced with a social fact "have-to" as in, "Kids have to start learning to read in kindergarten," we can challenge that thinking by going to counter-examples in our own experience, throughout history or across cultures.

Another key way to challenge social facts about kids and school is to turn to the empirical research on child development and cognitive science. Decades of carefully designed and implemented studies are there to help us strengthen our resolve about how kids best learn. Peer-reviewed scientific research on children's learning has flourished in recent decades, and although it is not without bias, cognitive and developmental science researchers lack any direct conflict of interest with early childhood educational institutions. They are helping us to understand the brain and mind purely for the sake of furthering knowledge. Social science experts use processes that hopefully limit bias and approach some sort of objectivity via the peer review process. We can hold that knowledge about children in our back pockets. It can bolster us. Along with our valuable first-hand experiences and intuitions, empirical science can be a powerful source of information on what we know about children and learning. This book is a call to make choices about parenting and educating children which are in synchrony with our best understanding about the ways their minds and brains develop.

What Is the Point of School?

The point of school is to grow deep learners, good people and engaged citizens. When we locate the meaning of early childhood education within a social justice framework, we prioritize social and emotional learning and intellectual development rather than a set of benchmarks. When we understand childhood this way, we remember that it is a time of life for developing core social dispositions rather than cramming for tests to come. Sometimes too heavy of a focus on academic skills can actually diminish the capacity for deep learning. Instead, schools need to prioritize thoughtful observation, reflection and planning on behalf of what is best for the child and for the community (Pelo, 2008). Once we have decided what we value in learners, then we can work backwards to arrive at the best curriculum and pedagogical goals.

Dr. Michael Palmer, director of the University of Virginia *Teaching Research Center*, is passionate about questioning the social facts of teaching and learning. He has examined how teachers usually design lessons and curricula and found that they often begin with imposed learning standards, or with textbooks and curriculum materials that have been handed to them. Most teachers lament, "How on earth am I going to get through all of this?" But hard-working and dedicated teachers jump in, subdivide the topics into lessons, map the lessons onto weeks and then decide what will be on the assessments. Teachers feel an incredible burden and are under immense pressure to meet the standards and outcomes.

Backward integrated design for learning turns that process on its head, starts with teachers' genuine goals for children and moves the other way. Dr. Palmer uses something called "The Dream Exercise" to get teachers to think more broadly about transformative learning.

> Imagine you have a group of dream students. They are engaged, they are perfectly behaved and they have perfect memories. Fill in this sentence: three to five years from now, my students will still know ____. Or they will be able to do ____. Or they will still find value in ____.

One teacher answered this way: "I want them to think of math as fun and interesting in its own right, not just practical … when they see a math story [online], I want them to click it" (Heath & Heath, 2017, p. 108). The others responded in kind. As it turns, out most teachers want their students to be curious, to take risks, to stand up for others and not oppress, to really listen well and really think carefully for themselves. They want them to be moved by lessons, to be great thinkers and active participants in their communities (Heath & Heath, 2017). Young children can readily do all of these things! We just need to design their school days around how their brains, bodies and minds are set up. When we optimize for how kids are, we empower them. We can follow their lead, toward the best outcomes. Empowering children means choosing what alights their passions and helps them most in their lives, not what is most familiar or most convenient. We can begin this revolution in small and meaningful ways, even if we aren't given ultimate freedom or time in our current school curricula. Tiny shifts in how we do things can subvert the top-down nature of the education system.

Why Kids Need to Enact Social Justice

More than anything, children of all ages desire to be a member of the community, to be someone "to be reckoned with" or "in the know." Children have survived and thrived by enmeshing themselves in complex social situations. They are constantly studying the world in intricate detail, angling to learn the social and cultural rules. And children quickly develop a very savvy internal moral sense. When we were young, we knew when things were unjust: when the mean older kids picked on a child with special needs, or when more privileged children opened and ransacked a poorer boy's lunchbox, we felt those injustices deeply, even if we could not articulate the complex feelings.

While we are waiting for young children to be developmentally ready to consider complex issues, they are already developing values and beliefs about them. We often underestimate young children's cognitive, affective and ethical capabilities. Their own lives and experiences can be used as a starting point for deepening their understanding of social justice. Try listening to themes embedded in children's play and conversations and you will hear ideas about identity and belonging, about community and relationships and fairness, like: "A boy can't be the mom when we play family"; "Why do you wear that on your head?" or "Why is your skin different from your mom's skin?" Children are fundamentally concerned with understanding their social and cultural worlds, and teachers and caregivers have a beautiful opportunity to join them in this pursuit, guiding them toward accurate and empathic knowledge. If we shy away from that opportunity, we leave children to figure out their questions on their own, coming to conclusions based on misinformation and cultural biases. It is our job to teach children to be human and humane; that is, to think, feel and act critically. When we engage with children in questions about identity and equity, we participate in the work of reshaping our society (Pelo, 2008).

It is important to remember that children will enact the harmful tropes and narratives of the wider culture. They will swiftly glean and take on the biases and discomforts of those around them because they are such experts and naturals at community-joining. For instance, by preschool age, several studies have shown that the majority of children (of any race) predict that a white child will "win the prize" or "win the checkers game," and a non-white child will "be reprimanded by the teacher" or "throw garbage on the floor." These biased attitudes may or may not correspond to the values of these children's parents or teachers. However, because many parents and teachers avoid the uncomfortable subject of racism, children develop such views from the implicit messages in the culture (Katz, 2003). Here's what can happen at school: the kids who have had an easier life are more likely to be coming from families with more economic resources, often the white kids. Privilege begets more privilege. Those kids have been groomed by parents with surplus time and energy to ask great questions, to have self-confidence and be creative. Then those kids get more social cache with peers and teachers, because their style reflects the values and style of the dominant culture. We have to push ourselves and our students into new and sometimes uncomfortable territory in order to first notice and then avoid this unfair recapitulation. We need to crack open old stories and stereotypes in order to develop the socioemotional and ethical acumen we want children to develop.

A Great Moment for Bold Imagination

There is no other profession in the world that directly or indirectly touches the lives of the people as teachers do. While we educators are not responsible for all that is good, bad or indifferent in our schools and society, we can certainly take a more active stance to fight for an ethical and just world (Nieto, 2003). We have the right to remain silent, but silence on issues of oppression and discrimination connotes agreement. Even though the thought of addressing issues like hate and oppression with young children is daunting, we cannot afford to remove ourselves from the difficult topics that all members of democracies need to confront (Schmidt, Armstrong & Everett, 2007). When we teachers become overwhelmed or uncomfortable, we tend to fall back on the tired, old "teaching scripts" from when we were in school (Himmele & Himmele, 2021). After all, most of us spent upwards of 20,000 hours as students (expert at taking in the values of the "culture of school") before we ever began the work of studying to be teachers. When we get nervous or unsure, we revert back to the old habits and ways of old-school teachers: more tropes, more top-down methods, more control. It is at these times that we inadvertently teach children how to behave. Children are masters at studying adults' actions and unspoken values. It is a much harder job to empower children than to follow a well-worn path. Empowering the children is far less predictable. It takes courage and faith in the learning process as well as in the kids (Schmidt, Armstrong & Everett, 2007).

Let us now turn to the ways we can empower children: in social collaboration, play and joy, with curious inquiry, autonomy and agency, time, embodied movement, questions and dialogue. Each of these nourishes in children the skills to be premier learners who notice and care for others and are engaged and active members of their communities. I invite you to consider what we now know about young children and to boldly imagine ways we can leverage their exquisite gifts.

References

Durkheim, E. (1938). *The rules of sociological method* (8th ed.). University of Chicago Press.

Gopnik, A., Griffiths, T. L., & Lucas, C. G. (2015). When younger learners can be better (or at least more open-minded) than older ones. *Current Directions in Psychological Science, 24*(2), 87–92. http://doi. org/10.1177/0963721414556653

Heath, C., & Heath, D. (2017). *The power of moments: Why certain experiences have extraordinary impact.* Simon & Schuster.

Himmele, P., & Himmele, W. (2021). *Why are we still doing that? Positive alternatives to problematic teaching practices.* ASCD.

Katz, P. A. (2003). Racists or tolerant multiculturalists? How do they begin? *American Psychologist, 58*(11), 897–909. https://doi.org/10.1037/0003-066X.58.11.897

Lee, C. D., Meltzoff, A. N., & Kuhl, P. K. (2020). The braid of human learning and development: Neuro-physiological processes and participation in cultural practices. In N. Nasir, C. D. Lee, R. Pea, & M. McKinney de Royston (Eds.), *Handbook of the cultural foundations of learning* (pp. 24–43). Routledge. https://doi.org/10.4324/9780203774977-3

Nieto, S. (2003). *What keeps teachers going?* Teachers College Press.

Pelo, A. (2008). *Embracing a vision of social justice in early childhood education.* Rethinking Schools Ltd.

Schmidt, R., Armstrong, L., & Everett. T. (2007). Teacher resistance to critical conversation: Exploring why teachers avoid difficult topics in their classrooms. *The NERA Journal, 43*(2), 49–55.

Snow, C. E., & Hoefnagel-Höhle, M. (1978). The critical period for language acquisition: Evidence from second language learning. *Child Development, 49*(4), 1114–1128. https://doi.org/10.2307/1128751

White-Schwoch, T., Woodruff Carr, K., Anderson, S., Strait, D. L., & Kraus, N. (2013). Older adults benefit from music training early in life: Biological evidence for long-term training-driven plasticity. *Journal of Neuroscience, 33*(45), 17667–17674. https://doi.org/10.1523/JNEUROSCI.2560-13.2013

1

Empowering Young Children to Be Social and Collaborative
How to Nourish Empathy, Understanding and Valuing Others

Children, like all humans, are social and collaborative creatures. Their brains have been optimized, through tens of thousands of years of evolution, to learn and grow and work together. The Bantu people, of central Africa put it this way: kids become who they are and who they are meant to be, as a result of "ubuntu" – connections with others (Bond, 2006). Ubuntu manifests when kids play with, observe and actively engage with each other. This is true for all of us – our deepest and most long-lasting knowledge is constructed together. We see evidence of ubuntu right from infancy, as the most impressive skills, like learning to understand and use human language, are gained via the community-joining urge (Ostroff, 2012). Continuing throughout childhood, young children learn about their worlds by engaging with other children. During the Covid-19 pandemic, children suffered immensely as a result of loneliness and social isolation, despite

DOI: 10.4324/9781003202875-2

dutifully completing their lessons online. I will never forget my 9-year-old daughter Sonia laying on her bed forlorn, day after day, during the height of the lockdown. We now know in a visceral way that kids need other kids in order to function. For our children to reach key cognitive and socioemotional milestones and for them to develop the skills of empathy, understanding, valuing others for social justice, we must prioritize the time they spend in social interaction.

Evolutionary and Developmental History of Collaboration

No other species has come close to transforming the world in the way humans have. For a long time, anthropologists believed that it was our larger brains – our smarts – that gave us this advantage. But new evidence is showing that the human brain triumphs as a social tool first and foremost. When it comes to learning, each individual person doesn't need to directly experience something new to "get it." Just watching and being tuned into someone else's skills allows us to share and stockpile their knowledge (Alemi, 2020; Harre, 2012). In fact, the size of the social group we identify with corresponds directly to the density of neurons in the frontal region of our brains, the orbital prefrontal cortex, which controls much of our complex cognition (Harre, 2012).

Synchrony: The Beginning of Empathy

Babies ensure their survival by being tuned in with others. In the womb, they begin to regulate their body movements and sleep/ wake cycles with their mothers, and after being born, infants match their breathing, heart rates and emotional states with caregivers. This is a reciprocal relationship: when a newborn's emotions change, their parents' skin conductance and diastolic blood pressure also change in response (Hatfield et al., 1994; Malatesta & Haviland, 1982). Cycling together connects babies to others in their worlds, making sure they are not left out of the social mix. Whenever a single newborn infant starts to cry in a hospital nursery, the other babies will quickly join in, in solidarity. I would have bet my life that my 1-year-old son, Alexei, would not nap at his childcare. It was a ten-step rigmarole to get him to fall asleep for a mere ten minutes at home. But alas, in a room full of other toddlers, he napped along for the full hour, every single day.

Like the Bantu concept of ubuntu, we need to look beyond the individual child to understand social development. Joint attention, following an other's gaze to know what's important, is one of infants' first social skills, occurring by just 3 to 4 months of age (Eisenberg et al., 2012). Next, young infants and children develop social referencing, gazing over to a caregiver or trusted other when faced with uncertain situations, in order to glean how to feel and respond. Social referencing is fully functional by 10 to 14 months old. When I was doing research with 10-month-old infants in the lab, every time the caregiver was at ease, the baby would happily complete our perceptual test, but if the mom or dad was even a tiny bit unsure or uncomfortable with the situation, the baby would read him or her, become upset and fail to complete the session. I would implore my lab assistants to make the parents of the baby feel completely welcome and relaxed, and the baby's experience would inevitably follow. Incidentally, dogs also use social referencing – they look back to their owners to see how to respond when people or situations are suspect. But wolves, who are less in tune with humans, do not (Miklosi et al., 2003). By their first birthday, infants figure out how to direct others' attention themselves and can use pointing and gestures to get their main points across (Johnson, 2005).

Humans survive and thrive by reading and interpreting the slightest changes in others' tone and body language, and by synchronizing body rhythms, movements and emotions in a shared experiential ecosystem (Franklin, 2019). We adapt to others' postures, facial expressions and gestures; we pick up our best friends' mannerisms, and we even match our footsteps with folks when we walk together (Burgoon et al., 1995). Likewise, audience members' heart rates and breathing rates slow down and speed up in sync when they share the experience of a movie or a play (Feehly, 2021). This is why concerts, theater and sporting events are so much more powerful live than they are viewed on a screen. And it is why a Zoom yoga class or religious service is rarely as transformative as a live one. It is a completely different experience for the brain – when we are together, electrical signals fluctuate in sync, creating a feeling of deep connection and "self-other merging" (Valencia & Froese, 2020). In one study, scientists measured the neural activity of pilots and co-pilots during a flight simulation. They exhibited high levels of inter-brain con-nectivity during takeoff and landing when they needed to act as a team, yet their brains did not sync up during the cruise phase of the flight when the two pilots acted independently (Toppi et al., 2016). Another study showed that neural synchroniza-tion occurred when people completed a puzzle together, but the levels dropped when either the same people completed identical puzzles individually, or when both watched other people finish a puzzle (Fishburn et al., 2018). Similarly, when musicians play together, they physically mimic one another's movements while repeating musical phrases and motifs. This synchronization enhances attention, motor coordination and a feeling of cohe-sion. Players adjust to one another's inner pace as they sense, follow and respond to what is happening (Rabinowitch et al., 2012). We are meant to cycle together. These synchronies create the emotional experience of affiliation and fondness; they let others know, "I am one of your people."

Synchrony is also a precursor of empathy. By alerting us to how other people are feeling, synchrony motivates us to take their perspectives. Neurological studies have shown that when we see facial expressions of pain, sadness or emotional distress on others, our own brains' pain centers respond as though we, too, feel it. Mirror neurons are responsible for this – essentially dissolving the barrier between us and other human beings and keeping us from harm by keeping us together (Hastings et al., 2007; Townsend et al., 2013). The deeply rooted synchrony that children share with others comes to impact how they respond to others' joy or suffering.

How Collaboration Facilitates and Deepens Learning

Learning by Joining Communities

We usually think of learning as being the result of teaching. But social situations are so powerful for children that they can glean the most complex skills without any explicit instruction at all. Think of how infants learn their native language. To understand and speak any language, a child must come to perceive and master over 80,000 lexical items (sounds that combine to form words). They do this by the tender age of 3. And yet none of the lexical items they use are explicitly taught. (No one says, "Add an -ing to make the verb a gerund, sweetie.") Babies learn their native language just by spending time with others using it – they are so extremely motivated to join the community of language users! Evidence shows that children can learn to read by the same mechanisms – merely being in tight community with other readers. Many kids around the world, including unschoolers and children at democratic schools, learn very effectively without instruction – these children learn to read in the same way that we all learned to talk, without ever being taught. For instance, the Sudbury Valley Schools have been graduating literate and highly successful children for more than 50 years, none of whom were ever given any instruction on reading (Gray, 2010). It's true of other complex skills, too. Children around the world learn how to build, grow, forage and cook food and to play musical instruments all by being together in social situations with others (Lancy, 2012; Lave & Wenger, 1991). In fact, direct teaching of key skills and knowledge is relatively infrequent outside of Western, educated, industrialized and democratic populations (Henrich et al., 2010; Lancy, 2010, 2016). In most of the world, kids can and do learn effortlessly by spending time with others.

Solving Problems Together in "The Zone"

Kids can also solve problems that are beyond their individual grasp when they work together. Actually, problem solving is most effective and beneficial when done with other kids. In order to tackle a problem together, children need to use their minds in very intricate ways. They need to coordinate a joint action plan that includes their own actions with those needed from the others. One study found that by age 3, children could do this by identifying and taking into account what a partner was contributing in a collaborative problem-solving task. By age 5, the kids could even predict their partner's actions (Warneken et al., 2014). In another study, researchers discovered that 5-year-olds struggled individually to understand the workings of a mechanical toy with multiple spinning gears, which moved interdependently. But when they played with the toy in pairs, the children had no trouble figuring out precisely which gears were doing what (Schulz & Bonawitz, 2007).

When kids work together to solve a problem with other children who are just a little more experienced or advanced, they get pulled to new heights of performance. For example, if one child is strong or tall or smart enough to get a rope up over the tree limb, the other child can fully collaborate in making a tree swing with her, and the next time he will be more likely to find a way to get the rope over the limb himself. This experience of doing together what one cannot do on their own adds the confidence and experience to try again. Tasks in one's "zone of proximal development" are those that are just a little bit too hard alone but can be achieved with help or encouragement. If you think about it, we learned so many things by watching older siblings and bigger kids doing them – emulating those kids, and then joining in. Doing things with help created a bridge to doing things on our own. Collaborating also greatly expands children's communication repertoires, as they must listen, explain and share ideas (Schmitz & Winskel, 2008). One study looked at children's behavior in a sociodramatic play center located in a kindergarten through second grade classroom. They found that the older kids (the literacy "experts") invited their younger peers into significantly more complex conversations and negotiations when collaborating (Stone & Christie, 1996).

Grouping kids based on age or skill level is a completely artificial convention – it is not at all how children have learned throughout evolutionary or developmental history. On the other hand, interaction with diverse others, by nature, moves children beyond existing understanding and abilities and provides scaffolding for their learning (Wood et al., 1976). In other words, school classrooms comprised of mixed-age and mixed-ability kids provide opportunities for all students to work in their zones of proximal development. The more experienced children crystalize their knowledge and gain understanding from instructing the less experienced children. Working together allows kids to process content information in greater depth, imitate others' strategies, come into contact with alternative views and construct new understandings. Varying expertise levels on skills and topics can give all kids an invitation to engage in activities that they might never try on their own (Stone & Christie, 1996). Classrooms should be mixed in terms of age and ability in order to let kids broaden their range of those peers they consider "like them." This is beneficial not just for learning, but also for growing into ethical people. Research shows that children in mixed-age classrooms show more prosocial behaviors than their counterparts in same-aged classrooms. They also are less lonely and isolated, and less aggressive over time (McClellan & Kinsey, 1997). Being part of a group that is mixed in age and ability gives kids the opportunity to see many children as part of the in-group.

Further, working with a partner on a collaborative task increases the time spent and perseverance on the task. In one experiment, the mere presence of a partner prevented kids from giving up on solving difficult problems (Forman & Cazden, 1998). In another study, 8-year-olds solving math puzzles together arrived at significantly more strategies for solving the problems, and when differing ideas or opinions arose, the children worked together to resolve the difference. Working together also led to greater metacognition, as the students were able to reflect on what they contributed in terms of strategies (Dekker et al., 2006). Even when taking tests, students perform better when they take them together! Not only that, but they remember more of the material after having been tested in a collaborative manner (Zimbardo et al., 2003). It is an unchecked social fact that assessment must be carried out on individual students. If they can learn better together, why not let them show their learning that way, as well?

The data is clear: when young kids work together in school, they reach higher heights both academically and socially. But whereas collaborative groups in the business realm spend months on "team building" to establish trust and understand group dynamics, in the education world, child collaborators are expected to be high functioning from the get-go. This, despite the fact that most of schooling for most children has been an individual endeavor. Although children are often seated in groups at school, those groups spend just a fraction of their time truly wrestling with genuine problems together. This is because teachers are almost always forced to focus on individual learning, indicating another mistaken social fact.

A group of British education researchers identified 980 children from 5 to 7 years of age and created a collaboration training program for half of them, with the other half as control participants. The kids in the experimental group worked on trusting and supporting one another, with games such as blind walking and mirroring with a partner. Next, they worked on communication skills like listening, explaining and sharing ideas – including partnered discussions of favorite activities, "what makes me happy, sad, etc." The third component of the training was joint problem solving and included collaborative drawings and creating co-operative shapes and letters. By the end of the academic year, the children that had had the training showed significantly higher academic attainment in reading and math, and increased motivation to work with others. They also showed significantly greater on-task focus and better communication with their partners. Those who worked within the collaborative approach also had fewer incidents of disruptive behavior and an increased ability to work without teacher direction. The team building exercises had long-lasting positive impacts, with the collaborative children taking responsibility for and joy in their own learning (Kutnick et al., 2008).

To develop positive group dynamics, Ananya Singh asks her second graders to collaborate to try to solve an impossible problem together, called the Toothpaste Challenge. Each group squeezes an entire tube of toothpaste out onto a tray, and then their job is to try and put it back in the tube using only toothpicks. At some point the kids realize that it can't truly be done, but the negotiations they use with one another, and the creative approaches they try, help them harness their collaborative skills for their next endeavor.

Collaboration Nourishes Social Justice via Empathy, Understanding and Valuing Others

Just as children are born to be social, they are also born to be pro-social, that is, motivated to help others. Already by 6 to 8 months of age, babies show empathy for others, which is indicated by their facial expressions, vocalizations and gestures, as well as their attempts to understand others' distress (Roth-Hanania et al., 2011). By the time of their first birthday, infants will point at an object to help a searching adult find it (Liszkowski et al., 2006). By 18 months old, toddlers will attempt to comfort someone who has gotten hurt and will help an other achieve their goals by fetching hard-to-reach objects or removing obstacles for them (Eisenberg & Miller, 1987; Vaish, 2009; Warneken & Tomasello, 2006). Over the course of the second year of life, children's empathic helping develops even further to include sharing with others, often even at significant cost to themselves (Brownell et al., 2009; Svetlova et al., 2010). By the time a child is 2 years of age, he or she will notice what someone else is distressed about and actively comfort someone suffering or struggling. In one interesting study, developmental scientists measured children's pupil dilation as an indicator of the stress they felt when seeing someone in need of help (having dropped a crayon they couldn't reach, or having dropped a can they were hoping to stack to complete a tower). They then measured how and when the stressful arousal was reduced. They discovered that 2-year-old children's sympathetic arousal was reduced either when they helped the person or when they saw someone else help. This research shows unequivocally that from a very early age, young children have genuine concern for the welfare of others (Hepach et al., 2012).

When somebody else is suffering and we feel empathy, the parts of our brain that correspond to our own suffering get activated, via mirror neurons. Brain imaging studies show overlapping brain activation patterns when we feel any strong emotions, and when we observe the same emotions in others (de Vignemont & Singer, 2006). In other words, we humans are never quite separate from one another. When we meet shared suffering with compassion, our brain's medial orbital frontal cortex registers a positive response. Compassion offers an escape from suffering by improving the situation. This is the neural basis for kindness.

In Japanese, the word for empathy ("omoiyari") extends past feeling and into action. It literally means "the ability and willingness to feel what others are feeling, to vicariously experience the pleasure or pain that they are undergoing, and to help them satisfy their wishes" (Beam, 2018, p. 47). Toddlers who witness someone being hurt or harmed will spring into action. In an important research study, when 18- to 24-month-olds witnessed someone get hurt or harmed in the past (e.g., saw their clay animal broken or their drawing ruined), then later witnessed that person's balloon accidentally floating away, they exhibited significantly more prosocial behaviors to that person, by giving them their own balloon, comforting them, trying to get help or dropping what they were doing and watching in a serious way (Viash et al., 2009).

As children grow, they are even more likely to help those whom they perceive as similar to themselves (Brewer & Gardner, 1996, Dovidio et al., 1997). Thus, there is a great need for children to see their peers, classmates, fellow humans as "like them," rather than as "other." Kids need to feel like they are a part of the group for both their own well-being and their empathy for others. That is why it is so important for children to identify with as many different cultures, abilities and styles of being early on. Similarity promotes empathic concern, which predicts helping behavior. Fifth grade special education teacher Theresa Amoriello (2018) believes that empathy begins when children notice and accept each other's similarities and differences. To get the children to see themselves and others as all having important gifts to contribute to the class, she plays a Compliments Snowball Fight game. The kids write their names on a piece of white paper and crumple it into a "snowball" and throw it toward someone across the room. When a child catches a snowball, he or she opens it up and writes something complimentary (and honest) about the person. The more specific, the more effective. Then, when children get their own snowball back, they see their own strengths from different perspectives.

Inclusive education benefits students with disabilities and other special needs, and also benefits students without those special needs, in the form of empathy. This lets children see diverse peers as part of their community: not reducing difference in a "colorblind" way, but rather broadening out with whom an individual child can identify. Thinking and learning together with lots of different people enhances academic achievement, social skills and social cohesion – skills that are especially beneficial for vulnerable groups of students. Research shows that typically developing children who are educated in inclusive programs with children with special education needs gain myriad skills. They exhibit increased respect, awareness and acceptance, develop fewer prejudices and learn to be more helpful and supportive toward people with disabilities. Children in inclusive classes also make more friendships with diverse kids and exhibit better theory of mind skills (Molina Roldán et al., 2021; Smogorzewska et al., 2020). Elementary teacher Kate Dillon finds that young children will show empathy to a child with different needs when they are explicitly told to be accepting by their teacher. However, it can be even more potent when children spontaneously help special needs peers without being directed. This helping behavior can be contagious among the children. In Ms. Dillon's class, one first-grader, Brayden, was having a hard time and being habitually disruptive. His classmate, Emma, noticed and went over to help him join the circle. Later in a game outside, three more children – inspired by Emma – helped Brayden get in the game, and someone handed him a ball when he hadn't been able to get a turn to play. As they play and work together, kids become less attached to one style of doing things. They learn to accommodate different views and begin to imagine more diverse approaches to real world problems. Empowering children via collaboration very quickly leads to a fairer and more equitable classroom, due to an increase in empathy and the natural capacity to share, understand and respond with care to the emotional states of others (Adolphs, 2009).

Sample Nourishment of Empathy, Understanding and Valuing Others

We can induce feelings of communion and empathy by encouraging children to imagine themselves in someone else's situation. For instance, when Los Angeles kindergarten teacher Kecia Robbins reads the book *The Fire Cat* by Esther Averill (1983), she first asks the children in her class to imagine that they are the kitten. In this book, a big feral cat with big paws and big ideas causes trouble in town because he has not yet found his purpose. He chases a kitten up a tree in his unease with himself. Until Mrs. Goodkind sees Pickles' potential, he is surely misunderstood and judged negatively. Perspective-taking gets kids to catch the stereotyping they may inadvertently put on outgroups. In one strategy, kids are asked to consider the other, imagining how they must feel ("Close your eyes and allow yourself to be that little kitten, afraid for your life as you are chased up a huge tree." "Now imagine that you are Pickles, so bored with domestic life and deeply misunderstood"). This strategy is often labeled "imagine other." In a second strategy, kids are asked to imagine themselves, in their own lives, experiencing similar emotions to the characters. ("I remember how awful I felt to be stuck in my house during Covid lockdown. I can imagine it would be even harder if we didn't have a backyard"). This strategy is often labeled "imagine self." Research showed that both types of perspective-taking led to increased feelings of empathic concern and, consequently, to an increased likelihood of limiting harm and offering help (Myers et al., 2013). Fictional stories in and of themselves can enhance children's empathy. This is because reading good fiction emotionally transports us into the story. Our brain's mirror system is then ignited, and we become more empathic. Two recent experiments showed that empathy increased in just one week when kids were highly engaged and emotionally transported into a fictional story. The effects of empathy were significantly greater than the effects after reading non-fiction stories, regardless of how powerful the stories were (Bal & Veltkamp, 2013). Getting carried away, connecting deeply with the characters and feeling for them (the hallmarks of a great story) was the key.

Another way to boost synchrony and thus increase empathy is to let kids make music together. One important study found that 4-year-olds enhanced their cooperative and helpful behavior following joint music-making (Kirschner & Tomasello, 2010). In another compelling experiment, three groups of children worked together on games that centered on musical and non-musical skills throughout an entire school year. The children were evaluated for their emotional empathy before and after the study. Results showed that those who had collaborated music-ally (using rhythm, musical improvisation and music compos-ition activities) had a substantial increase in empathy scores at the end of the school year (Rabinowitch et al., 2012). Noticing and working around others' actions and desires musically can strengthen the same parts of the brain responsible for emotional perspective-taking.

Of course, conflict is inevitable in human relationships. The same elements that affect global conflicts are also pre-sent in early childhood education contexts (Bickmore, 1999). But, cooperatively identifying problems and their solutions can help kids to develop skills to solve conflicts. In the field of peace psychology, conflict management and peace building are heralded as basic skills for human well-being and sur-vival, given today's pervasive threats to human rights. In one school, an art therapist and teacher teamed up to try the Native American concept of Circle Justice to raise kids' empathy and to develop their conflict resolution skills. This process of settling disputes collaboratively focuses on healing rather than punishing. With Circle Justice, healing begins with taking responsibility for actions (Mikaelsen, 2001). Teachers Mr. James and Ms. Gibbons began the process with the children by inventing a scenario that incorporated challenges similar to those faced by their students. The fictional backstory was set in a second-grade classroom similar to their own, with a boy named Sam and girl named Kathy. According to the story, Kathy was working on an art portfolio for admission to a special art summer camp. Sam was angry and jealous of Kathy because his mother always compared him to her. So, when no one was looking, he threw water on Kathy's art project. When Kathy came in and saw her ruined work, she ran over to it and slipped on the water. In the fall, she broke her arm. Sam was immediately accused of causing the fall even though no one witnessed the water spill. He denied having done it and was initially pleased that Kathy and he were now in the same circumstance, staying home all summer. After telling the story, Mr. James asked the students to form a circle of community, to decide how to deal with the fictional situation.

Next, he asked his students to role play the different characters in the story. Each student chose a pendant to wear so that everyone could identify the characters and roles for that day. Students who selected an observer role were asked to be reporters using worksheets with the words "I noticed that…" Participants spoke only when they were passed a feather. Holding the feather signified who had the floor, either to answer the question posed to the group or to pass. Roles included Sam's mother, Kathy's mother, the school principal, the vice principal and four students with diverse backgrounds and perspectives on the events. The next portion of the collaborative lesson was devoted to making art based on the theme of that week's discussion. All art was created in the form of a mandala or circle, which provided containment in the same way as did the physical circle for the role-play. Each session ended with a brief period for observers to relate their observations and for group members to offer comments about their experience.

The children took Sam and Kathy's situation quite seriously. "I think Sam needs more attention from home" and "Sam needs help" were observations from the second week. Remaining in the role freed the students to understand the complexity of the conflict began to empathize with their own Circle Justice characters, such as "Sam didn't want to hurt anybody" and "Kathy must feel alone." Trying on different roles or being an observer allowed students to think for themselves about the steps involved in resolving conflict (Gibbons, 2010). Students took on different points of view and learned cooperative strategies for problem solving in the process. At one point, it was suggested that Sam could spend his free time working for Kathy or could help other people in need. After a few weeks of immersing in the scenarios, the children playing Kathy and Sam were ready to be friends again. Excitement and understanding were palpable in the classroom during the final week of the Circle Justice group. Students gained an understanding of different points of view while strengthening their own unique responses.

Young kids will need practice at perspective taking and understanding others' views, especially when those views contradict their own. The skill of putting one's own thoughts and feelings aside is like a muscle that gets better with more use. But once children get some experience at taking multiple perspectives, they have lots of fun doing it. For a young child, sometimes understanding and valuing others' perspectives can be as simple as seeing from a different vantage point. In a very easy perspective-taking exercise, you can put two chairs facing one another and ask children to take turns describing what they see behind the other child's back. "I see two trees out the window, I see a green jacket on the floor, etc." Then, when the children switch places, they are asked to notice each thing that the other child pointed out, thereby seeing the mundane scene through someone else's eyes.

Kids especially love responding to social and emotional dilemmas, because they are hard at work dealing with these conflicts all day long. Try presenting social challenges and then asking the children to respond to them verbally or in writing or in art. For example, "Eniko fell during kickball and hurt her knee. José laughed when it happened, but stopped laughing when he realized Eniko was crying. Eniko's team lost the game because she got out at first base. What is Eniko thinking and feeling? What was José thinking and feeling at first, and what is he thinking and feeling now? What might Eniko's teammates be thinking and feeling?" or "Yesenia's family got a new puppy and she is excitedly telling the class about it. Jefferson has wanted a puppy for as long as he can remember but cannot get one because his brother is allergic to dogs. What is Yesenia thinking and feeling? What is Jefferson thinking and feeling?" Then, when a conflict or dilemma arises in the classroom, these tools are there at the ready.

In Sum

Infants and children are highly social beings right from birth. This has insured the survival of our species and is likely responsible for much of our cultural and technological advancement as humans. Kids learn the most complex knowledge and skills from their peers and families and social groups, by first synchronizing their biological systems with those of others, and then carefully observing and joining them in community. If we can design educational experiences for young children that work with this social collaborative brain and mind setup, we will find that children learn with ease all of the cognitive and social-emotional skills we want them to have. They will learn effortlessly and deeply, and their learning will be lasting. Further, once kids are practiced at learning and growing together, they will be primed for understanding, valuing and empathizing with their fellow humans in a fair and just manner. But this means we will have to get away from ingrained individualistic models, challenge the assumption that we are in competition with one another and reframe our education systems away from the mistaken social fact that learning should be solo, hard work.

References

Adolphs, R. (2009). The social brain: Neural basis of social knowledge. *Annual Review of Psychology*, *60*, 693–716. https://doi.org/10.1146/annurev.psych.60.110707.163514

Alemi, M. (2020). The human social brains. In *The amazing journey of reason*. Springer briefs in computer science. Springer. https://doi.org/10.1007/978-3-030-25962-4_4

Amoriello, T. (2018, July 6). Promoting empathy in an inclusive special education classroom. McGraw Hill: Inspired Ideas Blog. https://medium.com/inspired-ideas-prek12/promoting-empathy-in-an-inclusive-special-education-classroom-d185d0da8fbe

Averill, E. (1983). *The fire cat*. HarperCollins.

Bal, P. M., & Veltkamp, M. (2013). How does fiction reading influence empathy? An experimental investigation on the role of emotional transportation. *PLoS One*, *8*(1), e55341. https://doi.org/10.1371/journal.pone.0055341

Beam, C. (2018). *I feel you: The surprising power of extreme empathy*. Houghton Mifflin Harcourt.

Bickmore, K. (1999). Elementary curriculum about conflict resolution: Can children handle global politics? *Theory and Research in Social Education*, *27*, 45–69. https://doi.org/10.1080/00933104.1999.10505869

Bond, M. (2006). Love special: Reflections of the divine. *New Scientist*, *2549*. www.newscientist.com/issue/2549/

Brewer, M., & Gardner, W. (1996). Who is this "we"? Levels of collective identity. *Journal of Personality and Social Psychology*, *71*, 83–93. https://doi.org/10.1037/0022-3514.71.1.83

Brownell, C., Svetlova, M., & Nichols, S. (2009). To share or not to share: When do toddlers respond to another's needs? *Infancy*, *14*, 117–130. https://doi.org/10.1080/15250000802569868

Burgoon, J. K., Stern, L. A., & Dillman, L. (1995). *Interpersonal adaptation: Dyadic interaction patterns*. Cambridge University Press. https://doi.org/10.1017/CBO9780511720314

De Vignemont, F., & Singer, T. (2006). The empathic brain: how, when and why? *Trends in Cognitive Sciences*, *10*, 435–441. https://doi.org/10.1016/j.tics.2006.08.008

Dekker, R., Elshout-Mohr, M., & Wood, T. (2006). How children regulate their own collaborative learning. *Educational Studies in Mathematics*, *62*, 57–79. https://doi.org/10.1007/s10649-006-1688-4

Dovidio, J. F., Gaertner, S. L., Validzic, A., Motoka, K., Johnson, B., & Frazier, S. (1997). Extending the benefits of recategorization: Evaluations, self-disclosure and helping. *Journal of Experimental Social Psychology*, *33*, 401–420. https://doi.org/10.1006/jesp.1997.1327

Eisenberg, N., Huerta, S., & Edwards, A. (2012). Relations of empathy-related responding to children's and adolescents' social competence. In J. Decety (Ed.), *Empathy: From bench to bedside* (pp. 147–163). MIT Press.

Eisenberg, N., & Miller, P. A. (1987). The relation of empathy to prosocial and related behaviors. *Psychological Bulletin*, *101*, 91–119. https://doi.org/10.1037/0033-2909.101.1.91

Feehly, C. (2021, July 26). Brains might sync as people interact – and that could upend consciousness research. *Discover Magazine*. www.discovermagazine.com/mind/brains-might-sync-as-people-interact-and-that-could-upend-consciousness

Fishburn, F. A., Murty, V. P., Hlutkowsky, C. O., MacGillivray, C. E., Bemis, L. M., Murphy, M. E., Huppert, T. J., & Perlman, S. B. (2018). Putting our heads together: Interpersonal neural synchronization as a biological mechanism for shared intentionality. *Social Cognitive and Affective Neuroscience*, *13*(8), 841–849. https://doi.org/10.1093/scan/nsy060

Forman, E. A., & Cazden, C. B. (1998). Exploring Vygotskian perspectives in education: The cognitive value of peer interaction. In D. Faulkner, K. Littleton, & M. Woodhead (Eds.), *Learning relationships in the classroom* (pp. 189–206). Routledge.

Franklin, A. (2019). Emotional contagion: How we mimic the emotions of those similar to us. *Berkeley Scientific Journal*, 24(1). http://dx.doi.org/10.5070/BS3241046897

Gibbons, K. (2010). Circle justice: A creative arts approach to conflict resolution in the classroom. *Art Therapy: Journal of the American Art Therapy Association*, *27*(2), 84–89.

Gray, P. (2010, February 4). Children teach themselves to read. *Psychology Today*. www.psychologytoday.com/us/blog/freedom-learn/201002/children-teach-themselves-read

Harre, M. (2012). Social network size linked to brain size. *Scientific American*. www.scientificamerican.com/article/social-network-size-linked-brain-size/

Hastings, P. D., Utendale, W. T., & Sullivan, C. (2007). The socialization of prosocial development. In J. E. Grusec & P. D. Hastings (Eds.), *Handbook of socialization: Theory and research* (pp. 638–664). Guilford Press.

Hatfield, E., Cacioppo, J. T., & Rapson, R. L. (1994). *Emotional contagion*. Cambridge University Press.

Henrich, J., Heine, S. J., & Norenzayan, A. (2010). The weirdest people in the world? *Behavioral Brain Sciences, 33*(2–3), 61–83. https://doi.org/10.1017/S0140525X0999152X

Hepach, R., Vaish, A., & Tomasello, M. (2012). Young children are intrinsically motivated to see others helped. *Psychological Science, 23*, 967–972. https://doi.org/10.1177/0956797612440571

Johnson M. (2005). Subcortical face processing. *Nature Reviews Neuroscience, 6*, 766–774. https://doi.org/10.1038/nrn1766

Kirschner, S., & Tomasello, M. (2010). Joint music making promotes prosocial behavior in 4-year-old children. *Evolution and Human Behavior, 31*(5), 354–364. https://doi.org/10.1016/j.evolhumbehav.2010.04.004

Kutnick, P., Ota, C., & Berdondini, L. (2008). Improving the effects of group working in classrooms with young school-aged children: Facilitating attainment, interaction and classroom activity. *Learning and Instruction, 18*(1), 83–95. https://doi.org/10.1016/j.learninstruc.2006.12.002

Lancy, D. F. (2010). Learning from nobody: The limited role of teaching in folk models of children's development. *Childhood in the Past, 3*, 79–106. https://doi.org/10.1179/cip.2010.3.1.79

Lancy, D. F. (2012). The chore curriculum. In G. Spittler & M. Bourdillion (Eds.), *African children at work: Working and learning in growing up for life* (pp. 23–56). Lit Verlag.

Lancy, D. F. (2016). Teaching: Natural or cultural? In D. C. Geary & D. B. Berch (Eds.), *Evolutionary perspectives on education and child development* (pp. 33–65). Springer. https://doi.org/10.13140/RG.2.1.4151.7928

Lave, J., & Wenger, E. (1991). *Situated learning: Legitimate peripheral participation*. Cambridge University Press. https://doi.org/10.1017/CBO9780511815355

Liszkowski, U., Carpenter, M., Striano, T., & Tomasello, M. (2006). Twelve- and 18-month-olds point to provide information for others. *Journal of Cognition and Development, 7*(2), 173–187. https://doi.org/10.1207/s15327647jcd0702_2

Malatesta, C. X., & Haviland, J. M. (1982). Learning display rules: The socialization of emotion expression in infancy. *Child Development, 53*, 991–1003. https://doi.org/10.2307/1129139

McClellan, D. E., & Kinsey, S. (1997, April 3–5). *Children's social behavior in relationship to participation in mixed-age or same-age classrooms* [Paper presentation]. Biennial Meeting of the Society for Research in Child Development (SRCD), Washington, DC, United States.

Mikaelsen, B. (2001). *Touching spirit bear.* HarperCollins.

Miklosi, A., Kubinyi, E., Topal, J., Gacsi, M., Viranyi, Z., & Csanyi, V. (2003). A simple reason for a big difference: Wolves do not look back at humans, but dogs do. *Current Biology, 13*, 763–766. https://doi.org/10.1016/S0960-9822(03)00263-X

Molina Roldán, S., Marauri, J., Aubert, A., & Flecha R. (2021). How inclusive interactive learning environments benefit students without special needs. *Frontiers in Psychology, 12*, 1510. https://doi.org/10.3389/fpsyg.2021.661427

Myers, M. W., Laurent, S. M., & Hodges, S. D. (2013). Perspective taking instructions and self-other overlap: Different motives for helping. *Motivation and Emotion, 38*, 224–234. https://doi.org/10.1007/s11031-013-9377-y

Ostroff, W. L. (2012). *Understanding how young children learn: Bringing the science of child development to the classroom.* ASCD.

Rabinowitch, T. C., Cross, I., & Burnard, P. (2012). Long-term musical group interaction has a positive influence on empathy in children. *Psychology of Music, 41*(4), 484–498. https://doi.org/10.1177/0305735612440609

Roth-Hanania, R., Davidov, M., & Zahn-Waxler, C. (2011). Empathy development from 8 to 16 months: Early signs of concern for others. *Infant Behavior and Development, 34*, 447–458. https://doi.org/10.1016/j.infbeh.2011.04.007

Schulz, L. E., & Bonawitz, E. B. (2007). Serious fun: Preschoolers engage in more exploratory play when evidence is confounded.

Developmental Psychology, 43(4), 1045–1050. https://doi.org/10.1037/0012-1649.43.4.1045

Smogorzewska, J., Szumski, G., & Grygiel, P. (2020). Theory of mind goes to school: Does educational environment influence the development of theory of mind in middle childhood? *PLoS One, 15,* e0237524. https://doi.org/10.1371/journal.pone.0237524

Stone, S. J., & Christie, J. F. (1996). Collaborative literacy learning during sociodramatic play in a multiage (K-2) primary classroom. *Journal of Research in Childhood Education, 10*(2), 123–133. https://doi.org/10.1080/02568549609594895

Svetlova, M., Nichols, S. R., & Brownell, C. A. (2010). Toddlers' prosocial behavior: From instrumental to empathic to altruistic helping. *Child Development, 81*(6), 1814–1827. https://doi.org/10.1111/j.1467-8624.2010.01512.x

Toppi, J., Borghini, G., Petti, M., He, E. J., De Giusti, V., He, B., Astolfi, L., & Babiloni, F. (2016). Investigating cooperative behavior in ecological settings: An EEG hyperscanning study. *PLoS ONE, 11*(4), e0154236. https://doi.org/10.1371/journal.pone.0154236

Townsend, S. S. M., Kim, H. S., & Mesquita, B. (2013). Are you feeling what I'm feeling? Emotional similarity buffers stress. *Social Psychological and Personality Science, 5,* 526–533. https://doi.org/10.1177/1948550613511499

Vaish, A., Carpenter, M., & Tomasello, M. (2009). Sympathy through affective perspective taking and its relation to prosocial behavior in toddlers. *Developmental Psychology, 45,* 534–543. https://doi.org/10.1037/a0014322

Valencia, A. L., & Froese, T. (2020). What binds us? Inter-brain neural synchronization and its implications for theories of human consciousness, *Neuroscience of Consciousness, 2020*(1), niaa010. https://doi.org/10.1093/nc/niaa010

Warneken, F., & Tomasello, M. (2006). Altruistic helping in human infants and young chimpanzees. *Science, 311*(5765), 1301–1303. https://doi.org/10.1126/science.1121448

Warneken, F., Steinwender, J., Hamann, K., & Tomasello, M. (2014). Young children's planning in a collaborative problem-solving task. *Cognitive Development, 31,* 48–58. https://doi.org/10.1016/j.cogdev.2014.02.003

Wood, D., Bruner, J. S., & Ross, G. (1976). The role of tutoring in problem solving. *Child Psychology & Psychiatry & Allied Disciplines*, *17*(2), 89–100. https://doi.org/10.1111/j.1469-7610.1976.tb00381.x

Zimbardo, P. G., Butler, L. D., & Wolfe, V. A. (2003). Cooperative college examinations: More gain, less pain when students share information and grades. *The Journal of Experimental Education*, *71*(2), 101–125. https://doi.org/10.1080/00220970309602059

2

Empowering Young Children to Be Playful and Joyful
How to Nourish Flexibility, Sharing Power and Handling the Unpredictable

Letting young children play freely is the ultimate way to empower them. During play, kids can finally experience a world not driven by adults. They can be the teacher! They can be the baby tiger! They can bake 20 cakes, or permeate the earth's atmosphere on the reentry from the moon! In other words, playing kids have true agency, power and control – since all rules and boundaries are dynamic, expansive and determined by them. This type of freedom creates a joyful comfort with social complexity. In fact, play, laughter, pretend and silliness allow children to learn all of the skills they will need to be effective in the classroom and as engaged citizens in life: Ease with ambiguity, flexibility, sharing of power, switching gears and handling the unpredictable. Decades of research have shown that for young children, there is nothing more meaningful, nourishing or academically enriching than free play. It is the absolute best use of their time.

DOI: 10.4324/9781003202875-3

Evolutionary and Developmental History of Play

Babies first engage in sensorimotor play, when they use their little bodies and senses to test and experience what is possible. They may start repeating actions in rhythm, with banging that spoon on their highchair tray peaking around 6 months. Exploratory play emerges next. This open-ended play usually involves multiple objects for construction, stacking, manipulating and hiding things. Symbolic play, including pretend, is the signature and most complex form of play in early childhood. It begins around 18 months of age (around the time that kids begin to talk) and continues into middle childhood and beyond (Lillard, 2015).

Play is ubiquitous across cultures and species and is necessary for optimal development in animals and humans alike. If you look closely in the animal kingdom, you might just catch some Nile softshell turtles tossing balls into hoops, or juvenile red-bellied cooters in fake wrestling matches. Dart poison frogs love to flip each other around in rough and tumble ways. Monitor lizards will fetch sticks or shoes, while salt water crocodiles and Mormyrid fish whack tetherballs and freshwater stingrays play keep-a-way. Octopuses have been known to arrange Legos in fancy configurations and play catch using their jets and tentacles. Play is more than just a good time – across species, rough-and-tumble and chasing play develop physical skills; object play develops manipulative and cognitive skills; and social play develops socioemotional skills. Play becomes increasingly varied and more complex with age, providing practice for more advanced behaviors like planning and problem solving (Burghardt, 2014; Fredrickson, 2009).

What is perhaps most profound about playing is its resilience to circumstance. Children play in virtually all situations and will spend countless hours at it, never tiring of pretending, imagining, fantasizing, creating and inventing. I recently stood with a group of parents at the park, all of us lamenting that our children were not eating their lunches at school, arriving home at the end of each long day with untouched sandwiches and snacks (and wondering why they felt so grumpy)! We finally solved the puzzle: the children's play time outside at school was being coupled with their lunchtime. So, these kids had all chosen to forego food, no matter how hungry they were, in order to get more time for play. Even children with life threatening illnesses will prioritize play, despite how sick they may feel. One study found that playing was the number one way that terminally ill children wanted to spend their last precious hours (Aldiss et al., 2009). Children living through horrific and unimaginable war conditions, likewise, do not stop playing. Amid violent conflicts like the recent civil war in Syria, and in the Holocaust, children innovated ways to play. They somehow found a way, even if their games were pushed to secret annexes above a bombed-out building or to secure underground bunkers beneath a destroyed city (Feldman, 2019).

Playing is sheer joy to a child. Kids love to play. While playing, they describe the world as brighter and lighter, colors more vivid and physical movements more fluid. Smiles are difficult to suppress; laughter is contagious. Joyful play broadens kids' attention and thinking, opening them to a kind of floating, "do anything" feeling (Fredrickson, 2009). Grown-ups, when asked what true joy is, will often invoke childhood in their descriptions:

> When we do witness joy, more often than not we are a lucky witness to young children or to other animals, who seem to come by it naturally. Maybe that's because joy is often in some way "bodied," and these creatures are exceptionally bodied, which means their lived experience is kinesthetic, spatial, sensuously perceptive and present, among other things.
>
> Slicer, 2015, p. 3

How Play Facilitates and Deepens Learning

The truth is that play is the number one way for young children to learn. Play should not be an add-on if there is extra time, or a reward for good behavior. Play should be a priority of the school day all throughout childhood, because opportunities for children to play are concrete and measurable learning opportunities (Burke, 2010; Blasi & Hurwitz, 2002; Smidt, 2011). During play, children expand their use of expressive language; develop creativity and problem solving; develop their number sense and understanding of physics and mechanics. Playing combines imitation and synchrony with the complex, dynamic, free and unpredictable experiences that stimulate genes for nerve growth in the executive portion of the brain, the frontal cortex. In other words, play fosters activation of the centers of the brain that exert control over attention, emotion regulation and behavioral control – the very building blocks of deep learning.

One way that play incites learning directly is via exploration, uncovering new information or functionality. Right from infancy, exploratory play is linked with knowledge gain. In one experiment, researchers who observed just five minutes of free play in 1-year-old infants were able to predict their vocabulary size and risk profile at age 3. Those babies that explored more systematically and flexibly at 1 year of age had higher IQ scores later. Armed with this finding, we can create opportunities for inhibited and at-risk children to be able to explore, thereby bridging the gaps for them (Muentener et al., 2018). Indeed, one group of innovative pediatricians found that distributing building blocks to at-risk toddlers significantly increased their attention and language development skills in just six-months (Christakis et al., 2007).

Similar research shows that preschoolers who are allowed unstructured, free playtime with objects can in turn use them more effectively to solve problems. In several studies, children who were allowed to play freely with a complex toy developed significantly more knowledge about the toy's functions than those who were given instruction on how it worked (Cheyne & Rubin, 1983; Taffoni et al., 2014). Researchers have also compared the effectiveness of traditional versus play-based techniques for teaching math concepts to kindergarteners. The traditional math curriculum was led by the teacher, but the play-based program just let kids play freely with the same materials. After eight weeks, the kids who scored highest on mathematics assessments were those who learned by playing (Vogt et al., 2018). In another recent research project, preschool teachers in San Francisco conducted a close study of eight English second language learners, observing their language use at preschool for over 143 hours. The children came from homes where Japanese, Portuguese and Spanish were spoken. What they discovered is that the bilingual children learned vastly more relevant language information when they played with other kids freely, as opposed getting language lessons during teacher-structured, academic activities. The spontaneous and genuine back-and-forth, the authentic conversation while playing was what mattered for language mastery, and what was so obviously missing from the academic activities meant to teach language skills (Markova, 2017). Free play, here again, was essential to learning and scholastic development. The children knew what to do.

When we go for top-down instruction, we are working against children's natural proclivities to learn via play. Letting children freely explore is the fast track for them to approach, understand and solve problems. This has to do with allowing kids to focus their attention in their own ways, in effect, to make the knowledge their own. These studies add to a mountain of research showing that children learn more deeply when they are allowed to investigate via play versus when they are taught in the traditional top-down fashion. From building tools to retrieve an object (done more effectively when kids played with the materials than when they were given discrete instructions) (Cheyne & Rubin, 1983); to kids learning to use a computer in a hole in the wall (no instruction necessary) (Mitra, 2003), experimental cognitive science and education research show us that the best way for kids to learn is by playing.

Play Enhances Social Skills: A Pathway to Social Justice

One of the main reasons that play nourishes socially just behavior is that play immerses the child in a situation in which they can react in an unlimited number of ways, imagining infinite possible *new* situations, thus stretching their ideas, theories and behavior patterns. Playing becomes the arena for understanding and challenging the rules and goals themselves (Smidt, 2011). While playing, kids practice the social skills they will need to stand up for social justice. Examples include: negotiating rules with others in real time in real time ("How about only the captain of the ship can fly it?"), sharing power ("No – how about anyone with a magic stick can fly it?"), switching gears ("How about the ship lands on a mountain of candy?"), trying on different roles ("It's my turn to be the captain!"). This is sometimes called "storying" – the deep urge in our human race to create, make, tell and act out stories in attempts to understand our lives and concerns. When storying, kids shape narratives, try on multiple points of view, invent rules to hold the play together, negotiate with others, sequence events, decide outcomes and work out what is in their heads. Groups of children role playing must learn to work together in order to maintain intersubjectivity – an understanding of the feelings and intentions of one another other – in whatever play scenario they have created (Smidt, 2011). They need to find agreement for the game to proceed. In this way, play is much like democracy (Marano & Skenazy, 2011).

Play is a powerful mechanism for the development of self-regulation. Kids who can self-regulate can control their attention and behavior, including postponing their initial knee-jerk responses for more thoughtful long-term outcomes, and including initiating socially appropriate behaviors. In play, kids often need to self-regulate by inhibiting impulsive behavior and following emergent ideas; they need to slow down and deliberately act rather than react. Kids practice using language via ongoing dialogue with their playmates in order to resolve differences in perspectives, to reach an agreement about roles and to invent and follow the rules of the game (Savina, 2014). Self-regulation skills also activate the prefrontal cortex of the developing brain. These brain areas rapidly develop between 3 and 6 years of age and are linked to school achievement, social success and habits of mind that make them good citizens and proponents of social justice (Blair, 2002). Likewise, rough and tumble play activates those areas of the brain that work together to deal with social phenomena, including the orbitofrontal cortex, a brain area known to be involved in social discrimination and decision making. Playing physically with peers releases chemical growth factors in the social areas of the brain, promoting their growth and development (Pellis & Pellis, 2007).

Play is the primary way that kids develop the social skills required for peer relationships. In play, kids learn how to handle disruptions, negotiate disputes and dispel problems. They learn how to ask to join the game; to get their voices into ongoing discussions – which takes careful observation and cognitive sophistication. Hearing another kid say, "It's not your turn, go to the end of the line," is an infinitely better way to learn to wait than any admonishment a parent or teacher could give (Marano & Skenazy, 2011). Similarly, when playing, kids must enact the social negotiations needed to get into a game. When my niece Hannah moved to Spain for kindergarten, not knowing any Spanish at all, she simply asked her mom how to say, "Can I play?" This was what was needed to function socially.

Imaginative play is particularly beneficial to understanding others. Role-playing involves planning with other actors in real time, creating appropriate voices and actions and trying on the thoughts and feelings of the character one is playing (Brill, 2004). In one research study, preschoolers whose imaginative pretend play included impersonating others (playing the father or playing the teacher, for instance) were better at understanding others' emotions, over children who did not impersonate. Kids who were great pretenders were also more skilled at inferring and predicting the thoughts and feelings of others (Schwebel et al., 1999). Play awakens compassion and acceptance in children (Kolb & Kolb, 2010). More highly socially developed children become more empathic, more ethical people who are attuned to the well-being of the broader community, more prepared to participate in the civic arena (Souter, 2020).

Free to Play

Free play – free from meddling grown-ups, that is – is especially complex and beneficial for young children. Research shows that children use significantly more sophisticated language skills and more complex imaginative scenarios when they play in a group that *does not* include adults (Pellegrini & Holmes, 2006). No matter how much fun a game may be, when its directions come from the teacher, children consider it "work" (King, 1979). That is because the presence of an adult inevitably changes the power dynamics of the situation. Even the most well-meaning teachers often end up subtly telling children what to do, how to do things, where to do them and even with whom. Similarly, when adults incorporate play into learning, they often do so in a way that restricts agency, in which case the important developmental benefits of play can get lost (Dotson-Renta, 2016). As an illustration, consider this scene from a preschool dramatic play area. Four-year-olds Rahima and Joelle were playing with dough that had been put out amid some new kitchen tools, including a potato peeler, a garlic press and a plastic scoop. They invented a game that involved sculpting the dough into three different sized pieces and then sorting them into separate bowls. The dough pieces became coins with different monetary values. The kids were very focused on making sure that the coins were all of uniform size for their respective bowls, and they talked each other through this hard but necessary step in their game. Their teacher had her own learning goal for the children that morning: the development of fine motor skills with the new tools. When Rahima and Joelle had been playing intensely for well over 45 minutes, she came over to them and said,

> "Have you used that lovely peeler yet?" Neither child replied. She persevered, "Do you know how to use it? Shall I show you?" At that point Rahima grabbed Joelle by the elbow, whispered in his ear and the two went off to another part of the room, thus ending the complex game they had been completely and delightfully engaged in.
>
> Smidt, 2011, p. 9

On the other side of the coin, PlayCentre co-ops in New Zealand focus on child-led learning, with adults offering daily invitations to experiences such as building, baking, painting, dressing up and sand and water play, but letting children guide the action. Organizer and facilitator Cécile LePage said that children often choose to do things that require extra work in terms of clean-up, but at PlayCentre they can run with it because it is set up for that – things can spill, floors can be hosed down and children can be showered off; expansive ideas can be moved outside to the garden. In short, when genuine play is welcomed, kids' ideas might create a big mess, and that is okay because the cleanup is part of the work, too, with many hands taking responsibility for the entire process. One popular play invitation at PlayCentre is making potions. Here individual kids have their own big bowl (so that more introverted kids can do their own thing), but there are many materials and ingredients in the middle to share. If someone desires to get more expansive, they can move outside to the big tubs. Whereas adults tend to have their eyes on the scientific benefits of the potions, the recipes or end goals, the kids are much more into the process itself – they usually don't care about having something at the end, they are interested in the action of pouring, even if it is gross or messy. Sometimes kids want to pour everything they can find. Allowing this allows comfort with exploring. For many children who at first are uncomfortable or inhibited with their bodies or with textures, playing freely with potions allows them to become more comfortable in their own skin. If tidying up is made to be part of the play experience for a child, then that play can go big! (And the kids will get more out of it.) But if the grownups are the only tidy-uppers, then they will want to stop expanding play and exploration because it will cause too big of a mess.

Children may take a lesson in a completely different direction than we adults intend, because they may in fact be cognitively negotiating different things than we think they are. But teachers who take play seriously know that varying agendas are okay. We need to ask ourselves again, "Why must the lessons be always based on adults' agendas?" The best teachers are not attached to executing their plans. Like a dance, they allow it to take new forms; they guide and relinquish and even know when to step aside and let something more interesting happen. One way to do this is to only loosely structure children's time, as teachers at the Slate School do. During their Play and Play sessions, children can do whatever they want for 2–3 hours, as long as at some point they interface with certain materials, like books and musical instruments. Kids find their own ideas within this loose scaffolding. It is not unusual to see a group of children meandering in the Piney Woods, some under the trees with books scattered around, some ambling by playing recorders and some climbing high above.

Play Is at Risk

One day at breakfast recently, I asked my 10-year-old daughter Sonia what would happen if the children in her class could do whatever they wanted at school that day. "We would definitely choose recess all day," she decided. That sounded to me like the best possible use of time. But despite decades of research showing unequivocally that young children learn best when playing, parents and teachers still feel (and exert) pressure to make early years education more "academic." "They are just playing – when are they going to start learning something?" is a common refrain. This captures the devaluing of play and has caused it to be squeezed out of young children's education under the mis-guided view that learning is something delivered by teachers via academic work (Kolb & Kolb, 2010). Even for our preschoolers, play is being replaced by lessons on literacy and numeracy, to match content on upcoming standardized testing (Elkind, 2001). Indeed, U.S. children's time spent in unstructured play (both during and outside of school) has been declining over the last several decades due to an emphasis on accountability and stu-dent achievement (Miller & Almon, 2009; Hofferth & Sandberg, 2001; Stipek, 2006). Fear-based pressure is pushing children to achieve in ways that are not at all developmentally appropriate.

Such misguided fear has caused a massive and detrimental effect on human growth and development. I recently spoke with a former student of mine (now a first-grade teacher) about play in her classroom. She was wondering how to encourage play, when recess time is so short and also includes eating snack or lunch. "It's not like a I have a play kitchen or dramatic play area in my classroom," she lamented. But why not? According to the social facts of school, kindergarten classrooms get play areas whereas first grade cannot. In the two months between June and August, 5–6-year-old children are supposed to put away the "foolishness of play" and become academic since the focus of first grade is literacy, so the mainstream thinking goes. (Although the cognitive science research clearly shows the immense benefits to literacy skills from playing.) What is driving this sudden and ill-informed shift? Teachers feel pressure from their principals and heads of school, who in turn feel pressure from parents. And parents of young children feel the immense anxiety of the culture. Fear that their children will be "left behind" leads parents to view play and learning in binary terms, with play as peripheral to and less important than the acquisition of literacy and numeracy skills (Kane, 2016). This reveals a vast and tragic misconception of how children learn. It can be even more pronounced in preschool. Since parents are often regarded as the "customers" of early childhood programs, preschools are more likely to succumb to parental pressure and change curricula to reflect parental preferences, even if these preferences go against what we know about children's learning (Zigler & Bishop-Josef, 2006). Play, the most important, most fundamental feature of childhood is disappearing.

One driver of play's disappearance is that parents and education system administrators within capitalist cultures increasingly want certainty and efficiency. But learning does not work in the ways that businesses work. Tight management of time and avoidance of risk has negative impacts on children's growth, development and quality of life (Wyver et al., 2010). Limiting and eliminating recess is an emblematic example. Recess has been scaled back or cut altogether in many schools around the country. Nelly Torres was forced to mobilize as an activist and organizer when her daughter was struggling in the first grade. Her daughter's class had no recess at all and was being asked to sit for hours on end in their Chicago public school. Ms. Torres lobbied for the children to have a mere 10-minute break each day. When she was a child at the same neighborhood school, Ms. Torres had recess twice a day. "[Recess] taught me how to get along with others – whites and African-Americans played together. Nowadays, kids don't know how to socialize among other groups," she said (Adams, 2010). The trend can be traced back to standardized testing movements, which put pressure on school districts to show academic progress and forced them to squeeze as much instruction into each day as possible (Adams, 2010).

Recess time, increasingly seen as a privilege rather than a right, is least common in urban areas. Kids are less likely to have daily recess if they are African-American (39 percent don't have recess, compared to 15 percent of white children), if they are living below the poverty line (44 percent of poor children don't have recess versus 17 percent of others) or if they are struggling academically (25 percent of kids who scored below the mean on a standardized tests versus 15 percent who scored above the mean) (Adams, 2010). There is absolutely zero evidence that academic achievement increases when we keep children in the classroom longer, but there is ample evidence to show that when children have recess, they are less fidgety and focus more on their tasks; have improved memory and more focused attention; develop more brain connections; learn better negotiation skills; exercise leadership, teach games, take turns and learn to resolve conflicts; and are more physically active before and after school.

Another way to say this is that free play and other unstructured time is really integral to kids' learning, though uncomfortable for adults. In unstructured time, kids get to practice working through complex situations together. If we never let them do this, they never get to practice doing this. To answer the question, "Why can't young children have recess all day?" we have to say it is because of adults' fears and insecurities about learning. Because, as shown above, the research unequivocally shows that play is the ideal medium for deep learning in young children, making recess time the bona fide best learning segment of the school day.

How Playfulness and Joy Inspire Social Justice

Empowering young children is the way to reclaim the joy and playfulness in learning. Neuroscience research shows that surprise and novelty recruit brain areas that enhance joy but also engagement, attention and memory. This is a reminder that young children are not just under-developed adults – their school days need to maximize silliness, laughter, surprise and novelty, to open possibilities for authentic and lasting learning. We must cultivate schools where young children splash in puddles, take time to look at clouds and come home with paint in their hair, nurture friendships, hold other children's hands when they are sad, take risks, speak out against injustice and discuss and celebrate acts of kindness and peace (Souter, 2020). In new situations, kids can practice handling unpredictable events, behaviors and situations and develop skills of flexibility and acceptance, all powerful for cultivating a more justice-based and fair classroom community.

Joy is integral to a well-functioning classroom as well as to a healthy community and society. It is not just a feeling of pleasure. Joy is also present in the intensity of dealing with important topics (Meyer & Whitmore, 2011). Joy is present when a child sticks with a task that initially seemed daunting. Joy creates the desire to communicate and share with others – the sense that there is something important to be gained from every experience. Joy exists when a student sees meaning and application of learning to personal needs and goals, as a whole person in the world. This is what inspires a student to continue learning.

> There are moments when the students are so passionate and excited about a topic that I as the teacher have to get out of their way and trust them to shape the activity. It is in these moments that I come to appreciate that even I as an educated adult have much to learn from my first- and second-grade students.
>
> Wood-Kofonow, 2015, p. 24

When undertaking work for social justice, we need to always create space for being playful, having fun, for laughter and for celebration. Bringing play, celebration and laughter to the hard work of social justice brings oxygenation to the process. Indeed, laughing together is counterhegemonic; it is a way to access one's power, to engage in transgressions and take a leap away from the ties that bind the oppressed to the oppressor (Butterwick & Selman, 2009). When we laugh, shake our bellies, tears of joy in our eyes, these are bonding moments that bring life to a class-room (Butterwick & Selman, 2009). To take pleasure together is a powerful "tool" for building cohesion, cooperation, a sense of pleasure in being together – surely some of the necessary components to a cooperative effort of any kind. Humor can salve hurts and divisions; it can bring kids together and build community (Butterwick & Selman, 2009). Play, humor and enjoyment can reconnect us with our creative selves as well as with those around us.

Sample Nourishment of Joyful Flexibility, Sharing Power and Handling the Unpredictable

Improv is an ideal playful learning tool for engagement and social justice skills like flexibility, sharing power, switching gears and handling the unpredictable. Improv got its start in the United States as a vehicle for social change among Chicago's diverse immigrant populations. Group play helps individual participants to get more deeply in touch with their own intuition and illuminates absurdities that we regularly encounter in life. Improv is designed to both question authority and poke fun at rigid, conventional points of view by decentering traditional power structures (Felt & Greenberg, 2013). For example, at Irondale, a Brooklyn-based theatre group, local police officers and civilians use improv and acting techniques to build communication and empathy. In 10-week sessions, police officers and civilians learn and apply improv tools to "step into each other's shoes," grow mutual trust and cultivate empathetic understanding. But most of all they find their shared humanity through play and fun (Shulman, 2016)!

Children are ideal improvisers – they are playful, unselfconscious, imaginative and can get on board with an idea quickly (Bangert, 2020). In improv, suddenly the kids are the experts and the adults are the novices. No one is in charge because everyone must think and learn on their feet, treat scene partners as equals and play together, embracing permission to be silly and just play. Kids are constantly improvising, not only in play, but in language, singing, playing instruments, dance, movement and art, and it helps them learn (Connors, 2018). This destruction of traditional hierarchies, particularly where teachers and students are concerned, can be liberating and transformative for all parties.

Improv is fantastic for multimodal and embodied concept integration in young children. It helps them make ideas visceral. They may hear the word "wiggly," and even watch something wiggly, but if they move like a wiggly worm, they understand the concept in a more meaningful way. Standing as straight as a "candle on a birthday cake" helps them feel what the concept of "tall" means and integrate it into their thinking (Connors, 2018). And there are myriad other skills that improv nourishes in young learners. It bolsters creativity by encouraging kids to mix two or more ideas or genres together to create something new, for instance playing a drum (one idea) as quietly as a mouse (another idea) (Connors, 2018). Improvisation reinforces to children the idea that learning is collaborative – it is about using *everyone's* ideas. By creating together, you let others know that you value their ideas. By making things up and being ridiculous together, young children practice the security of knowing that even if we don't always know what is coming next, we are always on the same team (Bangert, 2020). Improv has also been known to help children become more articulate. Since you need to be able to effectively get your message across in a scene, kids become practiced at explaining their motives and concerns without resorting to things like crying or hitting.

One classic improv game to try with little ones is called "Yes, And Box." To play, pick up an imaginary box and say "This is a box" and pass it to a child. They will say "Yes! And – " and then add one thing to it and pass it to someone else. The idea is that you build off the last thing that was said, rather than just naming random things. For example: "This is a box." "Yes! And, there's there a puppy in the box." "Yes, and the puppy is eating pizza." "Yes, and the pizza is topped with hot dog slices!" The box can defy time, space, physics and history, so anything goes! This improv game builds collaborative and listening skills for young children. Plus, it allows silliness and play to build community, take multiple perspectives and level power dynamics.

A group of second graders at Slate School took this improv spirit even further by creating an imaginary land called "Yes, And," where everything was possible. First the children brainstormed their houses – both by the sea and next door in the mountains – anything they could dream up could exist in "Yes, And." Then the children created names for their characters, and decided together that nobody gets old there. When Kobe Bryant and his daughter died in a tragic helicopter accident, some kids immediately designed them a home in "Yes, And" as well. This piqued the children's interest in the creation story of their land, which carried them into a homegrown humanities lesson about diverse creation stories from other cultures. With the help of the U.S. Constitution and some pre-law students from local Quinnipiac University, these second graders considered immigration issues ("Was there infinite room for everyone?") and succeeded in drawing up a constitution for their land. What began as a snack table brainstorm took the form of a fully realized society, all documented in a big book of ideas and stories inviting child citizens to join in or revisit.

In Sum

Children are naturally playful. Playing is woven into the fabric of their brains and their bodies – its desire shows up right away in development, and it is robust across species and situations. And kids love to play! We can use this to our advantage as educators and raisers of kids. All of the skills we want them to gain are available right there in play. Rather than putting play on the back burner or holding play as a reward for hard work, we can situate play at the center of children's learning, as its foundation. Doing that will require some humility from us adults. It might enflame pushback from folks who want to run childhood education on a linear, efficient, industrial capitalist model. But we must trouble the pervasive cultural assumptions about how kids best learn and grow into responsible citizens. We have the research in our corner for this uncomfortable examination of our society's hidden social facts. Decades of studies have shown that play is the number one way for young children to learn, cognitively, physically and socio-emotionally. Playing with other children nourishes kids into ethical and just people who grow to become engaged, emergent citizens.

References

Adams, C. (2010). Recess makes kids smarter. *Instructor, 120*(5), 55–58.

Aldiss, S., Horstman, M., O'Leary, C., Richardson, A., & Gibson, F. (2009). What is important to young children who have cancer while in hospital? *Children & Society, 23*, 85–98. https://doi.org/10.1111/j.1099-0860.2008.00162.x

Bangert, C. (2020, April 13). "Yes, and": Miss Cynthia's guide to improv for you and your little ones. www.bubblesacademy.com/guide-to-improv-for-you-and-your-little-ones/

Blair, C. (2002). School readiness: Integrating cognition and emotion in a neurobiological conceptualization of children's functioning at school entry. *American Psychologist, 57*, 111–127. https://doi.org/10.1037/0003-066X.57.2.111

Blasi, M., & Hurwitz, S. C. (2002). For parents particularly: To be successful – Let them play! *Childhood Education, 79*(2), 101–102. https://doi.org/10.1080/00094056.2003.10522779

Brill, F. (2004). Thinking outside the box: Imagination and empathy beyond story writing. *Literacy, 38*, 83–89. https://doi.org/10.1111/j.0034-0472.2004.03802004.x

Burghardt, G. M. (2014). A brief glimpse at the long evolutionary history of play. *Animal Behavior and Cognition, 1*(2), 90–98. https://doi.org/10.12966/abc.05.01.2014

Burke, A. M. (2010). *Ready to learn: Using play to build literacy skills in young learners*. Pembroke Publishers.

Butterwick, S., & Selman, J. (2009). Shaking the belly: Laughter as "good medicine" in anti-oppressive work educational insights, *13*(2). http://ccfi.educ.ubc.ca/publication/insights/v13n02/toc.html

Cheyne, J. A., & Rubin, K. H. (1983). Playful precursors of problem solving in preschoolers. *Developmental Psychology, 19*(4), 577–584. https://doi.org/10.1037/0012-1649.19.4.577

Christakis, D. A., Zimmerman, F. J., & Garrison, M. M. (2007). Effect of block play on language acquisition and attention in toddlers. *Archives of Pediatrics & Adolescent Medicine*, *161*(10), 967–971. https://doi.org/10.1001/archpedi.161.10.967

Connors, A. (2018, September 13). 10 ways improvisation helps children learn. www.creativity-portal.com/articles/abby-connors/improvisation-helps-children-learn.html#.YXzWidnMIUo

Dotson-Renta, L. N. (2016, May 19). Why young kids learn through movement. *The Atlantic*. www.theatlantic.com/education

Elkind, D. (2001). Thinking about children's play: Play is not work, nor is work play. *Child Care Information Exchange*, *139*, 27–28.

Feldman, D. (2019). Children's play in the shadow of war. *American Journal of Play*, *11*(3), 288–307.

Felt, L. J., & Greenberg, E. (2013). Changing through laughter with "Laughter for a Change." *Occasional Paper Series*, 30. Retrieved from https://educate.bankstreet.edu/occasional-paper-series/vol2013/iss30/8

Fredrickson, B. L. (2009). Joy. In D. Sander & K. Scherer (Eds.), *The Oxford companion to emotion and the affective sciences* (p. 230). Oxford University Press.

Hofferth, S. L., & Sandberg, J. F. (2001). How American children spend their time. *Journal of Marriage and Family*, *63*(2), 295–308. https://doi.org/10.1111/j.1741-3737.2001.00295.x

Kane, N. (2016). The play-learning binary: U.S. parents' perceptions on preschool play in a neoliberal age. *Children & Society*, *30*, 290–301. http://doi.org/10.1111/chso.12140

King, N. R. (1979). Play: The kindergartners' perspective. *The Elementary School Journal*, *80*(2), 80–87.

Kolb, A. Y., & Kolb, D. A. (2010). Learning to play, playing to learn: A case study of a ludic learning space. *Journal of Organizational Change Management*, *23*(1), 26–50. https://doi.org/10.1108/09534811011017199

Lillard, A. S. (2015). The development of play. In R. M. Lerner (Ed.), *Handbook of child psychology and developmental science*. https://doi.org/10.1002/9781118963418.childpsy211

Marano, H. E., & Skenazy, L. (2011). Why parents should stop overprotecting kids and let them play. *American Journal of Play*, *3*(4), 423–442.

Markova, I. (2017). Effects of academic and non-academic instructional approaches on preschool English language learners' classroom engagement and English language development. *Journal of Early Childhood Research*, *15*(4), 339–358. https://doi.org/10.1177/1476718X15609390

Meyer, R. J., & Whitmore, K. F. (Eds.). (2011). *Reclaiming reading: Teachers, students, and researchers regaining spaces for thinking and action* (1st ed.). Routledge. https://doi.org/10.4324/9780203832660

Miller, E., & Almon, J. (2009). *Crisis in the kindergarten: Why children need to play in school*. Alliance for Childhood.

Mitra, S. (2003). Minimally invasive education: A progress report on the "hole-in-the-wall" experiments. *British Journal of Educational Technology*, *34*, 267–371.

Muentener, P., Herrig, E., & Schulz, L. (2018). The efficiency of infants' exploratory play is related to longer-term cognitive development. *Frontiers in Psychology*, *9*, 635. https://doi.org/10.3389/fpsyg.2018.00635

Pellegrini, A. D., & Holmes, R. M. (2006). The role of recess in primary school. In D. G. Singer, R. M. Golinkoff & K. Hirsh-Pasek (Eds.), *Play = learning: How play motivates and enhances children's cognitive and social-emotional growth* (pp. 36–53). Oxford University Press. https://doi.org/10.1093/acprof:oso/9780195304381.003.0003

Pellis, S. M., & Pellis, V. C. (2007). Rough-and-tumble play and the development of the social brain. *Current Directions in Psychological Science*, *16*(2), 95–98. https://doi.org/10.1111/j.1467-8721.2007.00483.x

Savina, E. (2014). Does play promote self-regulation in children? *Early Child Development and Care*, *184*(11), 1692–1705. https://doi.org/10.1080/03004430.2013.875541

Schwebel, D. C., Rosen, C. S., & Singer, J. L. (1999). Preschoolers' pretend play and theory of mind: The role of jointly constructed pretense. *British Journal of Developmental Psychology*, *17*(3), 333–348. https://doi.org/10.1348/026151099165320

Shulman, M. (2016, July 2). Improv for cops. *The New Yorker*.

Slicer, D. (2015). More joy. *Ethics & the Environment*, *20*(2), 1–23. www.jstor.org/stable/10.2979/ethicsenviro.20.2.1

Smidt, S. (2011). *Playing to learn: The role of play in the early years*. Routledge.

Soutter, M. (2020). Measuring joy: A social justice issue. Phi Delta Kappan. https://kappanonline.org/measuring-joy-social-justice-nonacademic-outcomes-soutter/

Stipek, D. (2006). No child left behind comes to preschool. *Elementary School Journal*, *106*, 455–466. https://doi.org/10.1086/505440

Taffoni, F., Tamilia, E., Focaroli, V., Formica, D., Ricci, L., Di Pino, G., Baldassarre, G., Mirolli, M., Guglielmelli, E., & Keller, F. (2014). Development of goal-directed action selection guided by intrinsic motivations: An experiment with children. *Experimental Brain Research*, *232*. https://doi.org/10.1007/s00221-014-3907-z

Vogt, F., Hauser, B., Stebler, R., Rechsteiner, K., & Urech, C. (2018). Learning through play – Pedagogy and learning outcomes in early childhood mathematics. *European Early Childhood Education Research Journal*, *26*(4), 589–603. https://doi.org/10.1080/1350293X.2018.1487160

Wood-Kofonow, K. F. (2015). The significance of joy in the learning process. California Institute of Integral Studies. ProQuest Dissertations Publishing, 3726279.

Wyver, S., Tranter, P., Naughton, G., Little, H., Sandseter, E. B. H., & Bundy, A. (2010). Ten ways to restrict children's freedom to play: The problem of surplus safety. *Contemporary Issues in Early Childhood*, *11*(3), 263–277. https://doi.org/10.2304/ciec.2010.11.3.263

Zigler, E. F., & Bishop-Josef, S. J. (2006). The cognitive child versus the whole child: lessons from 40 years of head start. In D. G. Singer, R. M. Golinkoff & K. Hirsh-Pasek (Eds.), *Play = learning: How play motivates and enhances children's cognitive and social-emotional growth* (pp. 15–35). Oxford University Press. https://doi.org/10.1093/acprof:oso/9780195304381.003.0002

3

Empowering Young Children to Be Curious Inquirers
How to Nourish Experimentation and Innovation

Little ones are into everything! They peek and poke; their hands are in the paint; they switch the lights off and on, off and on again; they are under the chair and opening the drawers. From an adult perspective, this may appear as a chaos to be controlled. But from a child's brain perspective, this is engrossing the sensory systems, minds and bodies in powerful learning experiences. Curious inquiry is the engine for deep and lasting learning. It springs forth from the biological novelty preference and is nourished by spontaneous and joyful experimentation and exploration in the perceptual realm. Curiosity changes the child's brain, priming them to engage, notice and remember in important ways. Inquiry – energetically seeking knowledge – is about trying to understand things that are not certain or clear; being inquisitive and not quickly making up one's mind. For a child to develop social justice-oriented habits, he or she must try to understand, and test things out, prior to acting. Great learners and citizens should also question all things (including social

DOI: 10.4324/9781003202875-4

facts) and systematically experiment with what is possible. It is this divergent thinking and challenging of assumptions that underpins every creative solution and innovation.

Evolutionary and Developmental History of Inquiry

Infants begin inquiring about their worlds right away. They look at, listen to or play with things they have never experienced before as an efficient way for their immature cognitive systems to process information. Novelty preference is a sign of robust development and health; it first helps babies survive by making sure that they pay attention to anything in the environment that can help or harm them (Lloyd-Fox et al., 2019). Almost all organisms with nervous systems show a novelty preference (Slater, 2004). Since needed information is almost always missing, our hunter-gatherer ancestors developed a pure hunger for information. Learning about the world is the best way to reduce its uncertainty (Cervera et al., 2020). In babies and kids, this develops into curiosity, the insatiable urge to explore and understand. In that way, young learners behave like scientists – constantly forming and testing hypotheses. They then revise their models and theories when they come upon new evidence. More exploratory children actually show superior cognitive skills. When 1-year-olds encounter ambiguities about objects, they pay them significantly more attention. They also show the same pupil dilation pattern that adults show when they make inferences using deductive reasoning (Cesana-Arlotti et al., 2018).

The strong desire to understand underlies all human knowledge. In one study, scientists found that by observing just one hour of infants' object exploration, they could predict those same kids' academic achievement at 14 years of age (Bornstein et al., 2013). Another study showed that preschool-aged children create implicit causal theories to explain and predict future events. For instance, when 4–6-year-olds were presented with a gear toy that could operate in two possible ways, they manipulated it in ways that specifically revealed what the toy could and could not do. The kids preferred to do things that would lead them to understand the underlying mechanism, not just to get a fun reaction (Lapidow & Walker, 2020). Understanding logical structures is a key part of the fabric of the human mind.

How Inquiry Facilitates and Deepens Learning: Curiosity and Questions

For kids, knowing starts with being curious about themselves and about the world. Before kids can talk, they wonder and search with their eyes, with their hands, with their bodies. But as soon as they can talk, they begin asking questions, and they do it with gusto! The number one type of question that toddlers and young children ask is "Why?" They want to know how ordinary things work, and about the nature of human existence. They want to know about friendship, love, identity, knowledge, beauty and reality. My curious and philosophical son Alexei just now asked me, as I was working on this book, "If you found out that not one person would ever read your book, would you still write it?" His question sliced directly to the heart of the existential meaning-making of this endeavor on which I have spent so much time! Children understand that life is full of puzzling features, and they often ask about aspects of the world that adults take for granted ("Why do we have numbers?" "Do birds cough?" "Can one planet swallow up another?" "Can Grandma be in two places at the same time?") (Lone & Burroughs, 2016). In one cognitive science study of children's questions, preschoolers were wired with recording devices throughout a typical day at home. They asked a whopping 76 information-seeking questions per hour on average, in search of both facts and explanations (with one child asking her exhausted mother 145 questions in that single hour!) (Chouinard et al., 2007).

The best thing we can do to help children learn is to take their questions seriously. The answers we give to them really matter. Research shows that adults' explanations to kids provided the crucial information for understanding new concepts (Frazier et al., 2009) (Kurkul & Corriveau, 2018). But caregivers and teachers sometimes ignore a child's question, provide answers that close up further questioning or offer an ineffective response, like "Because I said so" or "What a cute comment," missing the opportunity for genuine understanding. Preschool teacher and blogger Teacher Tom Hobson (2021) said it well: "We are surrounded by a world that neither understands nor respects young children. Oh sure, we find them cute, but even in that, there remains a dismissal of them as fully formed humans." We condescend, responding to children in a way that makes us feel superior to them. But each missed question is a lost chance for learning. It can be easy to forget how much serious thinking we did as children, so we must beware of patronizing children's attempts to engage in inquiry and articulate their perspectives. After all, it was in childhood that we began considering some of the deeper questions of our lives (Lone & Burroughs, 2016).

On the other hand, when we really engage with and contemplate children's questions, we let them know that they are valuable members of our social group. Thoughtful explanations provide children with more opportunities to ask questions. This has a marked impact: by the time children enter formal schooling, the ones whose parents and caregivers seized this opportunity to engage them in inquiry show significant advantages in cognition, and they also ask far more questions by school age. Several studies have shown that mothers from families with low socioeconomic status (SES) talk less often to children, to use a smaller vocabulary, are more directive and use prohibitory language that limits inquiry (e.g., "be quiet," "not now"). Of course, this is not their fault – these mothers have much higher stress and work significantly longer hours than their higher socioeconomic status counterparts (Hoff et al., 2002). But, to compound unfairness upon unfairness, lower SES children are being further set back by this. One research study found that 4-year-olds from middle-class families asked about double the number of questions than children from low SES families. Could it have been the uninviting responses kids got to their questioning, which led them to stop asking? Every child has so much to add, so much to say. Being an "asker" is privileged in school, putting lower SES children at even further disadvantage (Kurkul & Corriveau, 2018).

Even in the best-case scenarios, children's expressions of wonder, and especially their questions, decline dramatically once they entered formal schooling. Kids very swiftly absorb the message that their questions are not particularly welcome in school, that school is "answer centered." Teachers, too, are enculturated to ask the questions as a part of guiding the curriculum and pedagogy toward their goals. When a child is wondering about something in class, he or she has to broadcast uncertainty, in a culture that values certainty above all else. In a recent study, kids' anticipation about their peers' judgments was directly related to how much curiosity they enacted. More than half of the students felt afraid that their peers would respond negatively to their curiosity (Post & Walma van der Molen, 2018). Perceived negativity takes over quickly: questions decline with each year of formal schooling. One study found that by kindergarten, questions and other displays of inquiry averaged only about two to five times during any two-hour stretch (compared to 76 per hour at preschool age!). By the fifth grade, self-generated questioning and exploration were all completely gone! Most children were spending seven or more hours of their day in school without asking even one question and without taking part in even one behavior aimed at finding out something new (Engel, 2011). If the experience of schooling halts children's sense of wonder, their spirit to learn, their curiosity and their willingness to care for the human condition, we have not succeeded as educators, no matter how well our students do on standardized tests (Wolk, 2008).

But all hope is not lost! We can flip this script and empower kids' inquiry by simply letting students ask the important questions. When questions begin with the learner, there is an opportunity for much more authentic learning to take place (Lone & Burroughs, 2016). Teachers can encourage questioning by modeling it – by being sincere questioners themselves, instead of acting as though they have all the answers. In other words, teachers can empower young children by humbly taking part in genuine inquiry, thus creating a dynamic view of knowledge. In the best-case scenario, teachers can let children's own questions determine what topics will be explored in the curriculum. What genuinely interests and puzzles the kids can be the grist for the mill of their lessons. When children get the power to inquire and seek, they become self-motivated and actively begin to collect information by themselves (Komatsubara et al., 2018).

For example, when Slate School kindergarten teacher Haley Grover's class observed a dragonfly dancing around a pond, one child confidently announced facts about dragonflies to their classmates: "When it dips down in the water like that it's laying eggs…" A teacher used this chance to invite children's own questions: "What does that make you wonder about?" If this was met with blank stares, or the repeating of the same facts, the teacher would start to model inquiry: "I'm wondering why the dragonfly lays its eggs in the water." These kindergarteners have a wall in their classroom to display their wonderings. It doesn't take long before the children start regularly exclaiming, "I have a question to add to the Wonder Wall!" The teachers then encourage children to select topics from the Wonder Wall and put them in their own Wonder Books. In these, children record questions with the intention of following up on them and seeking answers. The children here see their teachers asking their own questions and admitting when they don't know the answers. Thus, the children at Slate School learn alongside their teachers, walking the learning journey together (Grover, 2022).

When kids are curious and excited, their brains release the neurotransmitter dopamine (causing joy), and they activate and strengthen the areas of their brain responsible for critical thinking, decision making and planning (i.e., the prefrontal cortex, seat of the executive functions) as well as the areas for memory (i.e., the hippocampus) (Cervera et al., 2020; Kang et al., 2009). Getting a child's brain into a curiosity mode makes their learning deeper, more nuanced and more long-lasting. As one study showed, when elementary school-aged students read books on topics they were already wondering about, they learned significantly more information, picked out more details and retained what they learned for longer periods of time (Engel, 2011).

The noble aim of putting children's curiosity above our own agendas takes some practice for educators. Oregon teacher Adam Devitt had to go back and rethink some of his favorite lessons with this in mind. In the past he had used a fun lesson on sinking or floating for kindergarten through second graders. The children were given a chart to record their collected data and were given clear, concise directions on the project. But after a long, arduous cleanup, Mr. Devitt was frustrated with some of his students. He asked them straight out why they were not filling in the chart and instead were just "playing around" for the entire class. The surprised children replied that they had been working hard the whole time.

What Mr. Devitt realized was that curious inquiry sometimes shows itself in nonlinear and unpredictable ways. What looked like "fooling around" or chaos to him was in fact a series of attempts among the children to make sense out of their wonderings. On the second day of the lesson, upon observing a different student experimenting, Mr. Devitt tried responding to the inquiry in a more welcoming and thought-provoking manner. Denny, a kindergartener, was pushing a two-liter bottle down into the water, overflowing the tub. He cringed as his teacher walked by, suddenly realizing that he was causing a spill. "No Denny, it's okay. What were you trying?" asked Mr. Devitt. "I wanted to see what would happen," replied Denny. "And what happened?" Denny said, "The water went over the side and made a big mess..." To which Mr. Devitt said, "I see that, but why did that happen? Why did the water overflow?" Denny said, "Cause when I went like this [pushing down on the water bottle], it [the bottle] took up lots of space and the water couldn't fit [in the tub], so it just overflowed." Danny reasoned correctly that the bottle must be taking up space and that is why there was no room for the water in the tub. This rule of physics was the goal of the lesson, and here was a student who discovered it in a deep and visceral way and was able to articulate it. "How much learning have I missed as a result of trying to keep everything neat and tidy?" wondered Mr. Devitt. By allowing these children to freely play, explore and follow personal wonderings, this teacher created a learning environment where students were motivated to make sense of what they were doing on their own. Following the messier, more nonlinear sinking and floating lesson (sans the worksheet), one of the kindergarten students, Christopher, went home and filled up the bathtub and got a bunch of things from around the house to see what would sink or float. Kids were not only continuing to inquire on their own, but shared their learning with family members in a free-choice setting. Genuine inquiry won the day (Devitt, 2011).

Outcomes of Curiosity: Divergent Thinking and Creativity

Children, just beginning to know who they are in the world, are beautifully unattached to what they can and can't do, think or say. Kids' openness to unusual possibilities and original perspectives is known as divergent thinking. Divergent thinkers can generate a huge variety of solutions to any given problem. They can do this fluently and with originality (Guilford, 1968). A classic divergent thinking test might say, "Name all of the things you can do with a paperclip" to which a child is apt to ask something like, "What if the paperclip is 10 feet tall?" In fact, when asked these types of creative solution questions, children often come up with valid answers in the hundreds, while adults usually exhaust their ideas at a dozen or so (Robinson, 2008). Kids easily challenge and question not just the concepts and things around them, but the very frameworks of reality and knowledge itself. Divergent thinking is tantamount to creative problem solving, since challenging ideas flexibly can allow for significantly more spontaneous insights and "aha" moments. My son Alexei wondered at age 8, "Do trees feel pain when they are cut down?" This sounded naïve at first, almost silly. However, just weeks later I read of a study in which a University of British Columbia botanist discovered that when a tree is cut, it sends out electrical signals in a nearly identical way to wounded human tissue (Simard, 2018). Recent evidence from forestry science also indicates that trees can remember, communicate with and protect one another! We need divergent thinkers in order to push the artificial boundaries in science, art and human understanding. Kids' inclination to take risks like this amounts to a powerful learning strategy. It is why year after year kindergarteners beat out Harvard MBA students in the *Marshmallow Challenge*, to build in 9 minutes, the tallest freestanding tower out of dry spaghetti, tape, string and a single marshmallow (Berger, 2014).

Being less subject to adult inhibitions also makes kids better at certain types of decision-making. In one experiment, children and adults responded to a logic problem. While adults fell prey to short cuts and emotion-based heuristics in their decisions, children were able to see the problems without bias, and they outperformed the adults (Furlan et al., 2013). Most adults have gotten so good at shortcuts that they sacrifice good thinking for speed. But adult automatic processing uses completely different brain regions than slower more careful consideration does (Luo et al., 2008). From the Zen Buddhist perspective, kids embody "beginner's mind," uncluttered by preconceptions or prejudices, free of ingrained and habitual thinking and also free from doubt, where each new experience is seen with fresh eyes. As the Zen Master said, "In the beginner's mind, there are many possibilities; in the expert's mind, there are few" (Suzuki, 1973, p. 21). Kids have the beautiful ability to look at the same stuff we all see every day and see it with fresh eyes – that's how they're able to notice and comment on all the little quirks and curiosities that the rest of us miss. This is key for social justice issues. When thinking divergently, kids can look at old, entrenched problems and challenges for the first time, they are better able to ask fundamental questions that can sometimes get to the heart of the issue and yield profound insights (Berger, 2015).

Conversely, when we adults script everything, we can limit the chances for divergent thinking. That is why it is so important to create enough time in the day for idea work to happen (the insights, the new thoughts) as opposed to busy work. Educators learned during the Covid-19 pandemic that we had to let go of certain content because we couldn't keep elementary school students on Zoom for 6 hours straight. We had to whittle our lessons down to cover only the most important things. This was an important reminder, that idea work *is* the most important work; the stuff that comes from inquiry, curiosity and divergent thinking. We must try to sneak this in every day. Let something else go. Make sure we do the idea work first – make sure it's at the center of our lesson planning (Engel, 2021).

Teachers and caregivers' views on curiosity and creativity impact whether they are nourished or squashed. When teachers believe that particular children are more creative, those same children do become more creative and show as stronger divergent thinkers. In one study, preschoolers were much more likely to explore new, unusual environments in the presence of warm and supportive adults than they were with critical or aloof adults (Moore & Bulbulian, 1976). In a related study, children were significantly more likely to curiously engage in a museum exhibit when teachers encouraged from the sidelines, used non-controlling language and encouraged the children's autonomy (Eckes et al., 2018). Likewise, the number one predictor of how elementary-aged students actively investigated a curiosity box (a big cabinet with 18 drawers containing never-before-seen items) was the teacher's orientation toward curiosity. When their teacher smiled and encouraged it, children felt invited to use their bodies and minds to investigate. When the classroom was less open to curiosity, it was notably absent (Engel, 2011). Another study found that kids working with a curious, enthusiastic and experimental teacher were significantly more likely to keep experimenting with the materials (and continue their learning) during a free period (Engel & Randall, 2009). Remember, when we script or schedule children's experiences, we are depriving them of opportunities to develop and practice inquiry, investigation, divergent thinking and problem solving. However, when we open up their possible experiences, kids become curious, creative and divergent in kind.

How Curiosity Inspires Social Justice

We want kids to think divergently and curiously about even the trickiest topics. We want them to seek understanding and hold their minds open, to question those things that are so often taken for granted, especially those things that are unjust or unfair. When kids are skilled and seasoned at inquiry, they know in a deep way that it is okay to ask anything, and that they should always challenge givens and speak their true and authentic questions. In his children's book, *It's Ok to Ask* (2021), author Temi Diaz reflects upon all of the things that he was wondering about as a kid, but that grown-ups ignored. He then realizes for himself that while not everybody is curious to learn, the people who do take "the whys" seriously are the ones who make the world a better place.

Serious inquiry is key to becoming ethical, virtuous people in a complex world. The question is perhaps the most important tool for learners: it is like the spade that helps us dig for truth, or the flashlight that illuminates surrounding darkness. Inquiring helps us learn, explore the unknown and adapt to change (Berger, 2015). When they learn to guide their own inquiry effectively, kids become even more engaged and joyful learners. But, perhaps more importantly, they become agents of a participatory democratic society, able to contribute to civic life. Children who are adept questioners feel greater power and confidence. Asking helps kids assess things they see in the news, online and on social media. It will also allow them to make their voices heard and at the same time listen to the voices of others; to gather information, think for themselves and come up with solutions; to frame problems and challenges in a way that leads to action (Right Question Institute, n.d.). By encouraging children to query what they see or experience, we are helping them take early and key steps to gain some control over their lives. In a fully democratic society, everyone has a given and protected right to ask questions and seek answers. The answers may not always come as easily, but by taking our first, tentative steps to seek them out, we are on the way to finding out truths that are important to us (Zimmerman, n.d.).

In order to allow their inquiry skills to flourish, we need both to trust children and to be open and honest with them. What we sometimes do in the name of "protecting children" can really be serving to protect ourselves from embarrassment, controversy or the uncomfortable inner reflection that kids can raise (Sears, 2009). While young children have many as yet unformed views of the world, they are also very comfortable with complexity, sometimes more so than adults. A friend of mine who has muscular dystrophy and is in a wheelchair told me that in public places adults most often avoid looking her in the eye and very rarely say hello. But children often approach her and ask, "What happened? Why can't you walk?" She finds this so genuinely kind, and so welcomed. It is not all received how their apologetic parents imagine. Under the guise of protecting children, we can put them at risk of looking the other way at injustice, at avoiding conflict, at becoming bullies or being bullied. This also risks them developing dysfunctional coping behaviors and risks them not realizing their full humanness.

Adults often wonder: "Aren't tough topics like prejudice and discrimination adult issues?" "Why would we ruin kids' innocent experiences by bringing them into this?" Teachers, too, often want to shield kids from the dangerous, outside world and feel that they can help kids by preventing ethical dilemmas from breaching classroom walls (Schmidt et al., 2007). Some believe that we should keep a classroom a "safe" or neutral space and ignore tough societal issues in order to protect and keep students from harm. Again, the child development research can shed some light on this tricky topic. Keeping silent ultimately hurts children. The realities of prejudice and discrimination affect children's development very early. It is not only developmentally appropriate but also crucial to address thorny topics in our work with young children (Derman-Sparks et al., 2020). Children who are not invited into the complexity will still receive harmful implicit messages that lead to recreating biases in their worlds. Just as we do not wait until a child asks questions about how to read before planning how to provide a range of literacy learning opportunities, anti-bias teaching should be integrated in children's education from the get-go (Derman-Sparks et al., 2020).

Kids most of all long to be "in the know" – to be full members of their communities. They don't want sanitized versions of stories or to be told, "That information is not for kids." Much of what we believe to be beyond children's interests or understanding is actually not. Kids demonstrate serious interest in immigration, war, fair trade, animal testing and politics (to name a few), and yet discourses of children as innocent, vulnerable and needing protection dominate. This blocks children's access to information rather than engaging them in critical contemporary issues (Carter et al., 2009). When histories are presented in ways that protect children from unpleasant realities, they severely limit children's learning and relegate their understanding to linear and singular categories.

Adults sometimes brush off or ignore children's attempts to understand how and why people look or act differently from one another by saying "We are all the same. We are all friends here!"

Tropes like this leave the child to figure out for herself why the people around her seem different from one another. With insufficient information, she may well decide that dark skin means different kinds of blood, or worthy versus unworthy character. Similarly, when adults go silent or get embarrassed about things that children are seeing and trying to understand, children absorb the emotional message that the subject is taboo and should not be talked about. This undercurrent of anxiety and unease comes to underlie bias and fear.

Avoiding complex questions such as these came to a head at the Little Children's School in New York City. "Okay, now you are going to be my slaves," instructed first grader Joey as he grabbed the hands of two of his African-American classmates. The three children were playing together during recess, just having learned about Harriet Tubman. Genevieve and Rhonda, mothers of the two African-American girls, came to school the next morning enraged over what their daughters told them. "I was a slave today. Today, Joey made me a slave." Word spread fast. First-grade parents were ignited into a frenzy, and a tornado of blaming and accusations ensued. While some parents blamed the teacher for not sufficiently addressing the gravity of the subject, others felt slavery had no place in the first-grade classroom (Sonu, 2020). One thing was clear: the children were playing to try to understand and inquire about the history and unresolved conflicts of race in the United States. Adults blocked that inquiry and used a variety of different defenses rather than confronting the trauma and shame to get to the authentic engagement needed for healing. The possibility for dialogue or reconciliation was halted swiftly, and a series of public apologies were made, ensuring that there would be no future conversations on this complex topic (Sonu, 2020). And, of course, the silence also forced children to rely on unreliable information sources such as other children or the media (both major sources of inaccurate and often stereotyped information) to try and understand how they should feel about racism and slavery (Derman-Sparks et al., 2020).

Learning how to break such silences and taboos, how to invite questions about social justice issues with clarity, courage and caring, is an essential skill for educators (Derman-Sparks et al., 2020). The more open the environment, the more likely children will ask their sincere questions. This includes asking critical questions about stereotypes, prejudice and discrimination. After all, infants develop conceptions of race at an extremely young age, preferring faces of their own race by 3 months old (Kelly et al., 2005). Studies stretching back to the 1940s show that preschoolers readily absorb biased, discriminatory and prejudiced views. By the time children start school, their perceptions of difference largely reflect and perpetuate the dominant racialized, gendered, sexualized, classed and body stereotypes and prejudices that prevail in the broader society (Robinson & Jones Díaz, 2016). Children as young as 5 years of age predict, for example, that an Asian student would outperform a white student on a math exam (Ambady et al., 2001). Too often, stereotypes impact children from marginalized communities and shape their feelings of themselves. This leads to uncertainty about whether they belong and can adversely impact their motivation to learn (Walton & Cohen, 2011). In all classroom activities, we need to let kids ask about difference and complexity and we need to match their earnest questions a tone of sincere interest.

Sample Nourishment of Experimentation and Innovation

Some of the most impactful innovations are those that change our thinking. Critically thinking about society's challenges gives us the opportunity to turn something that is "unfair" into something more closely approaching "fair." This can involve addressing personal conflict, or helping a child speak up for another child. But it is particularly powerful when children question systems of injustice together (Derman-Sparks et al., 2020). For example, teachers at the Garden of Learning and Discovery Pre-K Center in Highbridge, Bronx recently decided to problematize global water accessibility and conservation within their learning community. They began this inquiry in school by counting plastic water bottles and asking when and why people used them. Then they began holding informative sessions for families and asking the entire community to participate in a reusable water-bottle challenge. Their desire was to get everyone to question and challenge their own unconscious behaviors. They then raised awareness about the scarcity of water throughout the world, making sure that the children knew that there are 3-, 4- and 5-year-olds that have to walk miles every single day for a luxury that these students just had to turn the faucet to obtain. As the children became more invested, more inquisitive and ultimately more knowledgeable about the plight of others, teachers began to see an increase in the level of empathy shown toward their peers and a desire to bring change to their community as a whole (Benavides et al., 2020).

In 2019, the school culminated their authentic inquiry project with a Walk for Water. Joined by students, staff, families and community members, they walked across the High Bridge, a historical aqueduct that once transported water between Manhattan and the Bronx, to bring awareness to the global water crisis. The school partnered with the We Movement, a social activism organization that has grown in response to the knowledge that more than 840 million people worldwide are living without access to clean water and that 40 percent of the world's population is affected by water scarcity. The community supported the tiny activists with cheerful applause and genuine surprise and delight at the thunder of preschoolers' feet that passed their buildings. At that moment, the students joined the ranks of other young social justice organizers in history, totaling 90 4 and 5-year-olds participating. The Walk for Water was a first answer to months of asking, probing and introspection. One community member reflected, "The children may be small, but their message is big!" A teacher commented, "The transformation in engagement and agency is clear. Kids are never too young to learn about activism and social justice. Our children now know their voices matter and that they can make a difference." This community realized that early childhood is the perfect time to begin questioning the way things are and establishing a collective mindset. As early childhood educators, we can introduce this important work organically, to weave it throughout our instruction and interactions, and to ensure it is developmentally appropriate. Indeed, it is not too early to provide our youngest learners with the tools necessary to become questioners of what is okay and not okay; to be environmental advocates and global ambassadors. Rather than shying away from tough topics, they should be an integral part of what is learned in early childhood. A knowledge-rich and action-oriented education lays the foundation for an indestructible and more equitable society (Benavides et al., 2020).

In Sum

Curiosity provides children with opportunities for seeking, practicing and refining new abilities, making it *the* driving force behind the acquisition of skills and knowledge. Young children are ineffably curious, and their best learning begins with their own interests. This is because authentic inquiry activates the dopaminergic system of the brain, enhancing attention and memory. Getting the child's brain into such a "curiosity state" makes their learning deeper, more nuanced, broad and longer-lasting. Curiosity in young children often manifests in questions, which decline dramatically as they go through school. But when their questions are honored and their ideas considered, kids burst forth with divergent thinking and creativity. Curious inquiry inspires social justice by strengthening the habits of mind of questioning the injustices in our political and social milieus. Fantasies of childhood innocence ultimately harm children more than helping them, because they engender silence and halt practice with handling complexity. Most of all, children want to be taken seriously as thinkers and actors in their communities. When we teach children to confront social justice issues, their ideas can evolve into the deeper experimentation and innovation we need in order to make the world a fairer and more just place for all.

References

Ambady, N., Shih, M., Kim, A., & Pittinsky, T.L. (2001). Stereotype susceptibility in children: Effects of identity activation on quantitative performance. *Psychological Science*, *12*(5), 385–390. https://doi. org/10.1111/1467-9280.00371

Benavides, V., Ledda, R., & Mohammed, M. (2020). Never too young to support a cause: Supporting positive identity development through social justice curriculum in preschool. *Young Children*, *75*(5), 14–19.

Berger, W. (2014). *A more beautiful question*. Bloomsbury.

Berger, W. (2015, August 17). 5 ways to help your students become better questioners. www.edutopia.org/blog/help-students-become-better-questioners-warren-berger

Bornstein, M. H., Hahn, C. S., & Suwalsky, J. T. (2013). Physically developed and exploratory young infants contribute to their own long-term academic achievement. *Psychological Science*, *24*, 1906–1917. https://doi.org/10.1177/0956797613479974

Carter, C., Messenger Davies, M., Allan, S., Mendes, K., Milani, R., & Wass, L. (2009). What do children want from the BBC? Children's content and participatory environments in an age of citizen media. BBC. www.bbc.co.uk/blogs/knowledgeexchange/cardifftwo.pdf

Cervera, R. L., Wang, M. Z., & Hayden, B. Y. (2020). Systems neuroscience of curiosity. *Current Opinion in Behavioral Sciences*, *35*, 48–55. https://doi.org/10.1016/j.cobeha.2020.06.011

Cesana-Arlotti, N., Martín, A., Téglás, E., Vorobyova, L., Cetnarski, R., & Bonatti, L.L. (2018). Precursors of logical reasoning in preverbal human infants. *Science*, *359*, 1263–1266. https://doi.org/10.1126/science.aao3539

Chouinard, M. (2007). Children's questions: A mechanism for cognitive development [Monograph]. *Monographs of the Society for Research in Child Development*, *72*, vii–ix. https://doi.org/10.1111/j.1540-5834.2007.00412.x

Derman-Sparks, L., Edwards, J. O., & Goins, C.M. (2020). *Anti-bias education for young children and ourselves* (2nd ed). NAEYC.

Devitt, A. (2011). Capitalizing on curiosity: The pursuit for understanding the science during children's inquiry experiences. *Science and Children*, *48*(9), 44–47.

Diaz, T. (2021). *It's ok to ask: A book to promote kids' critical thinking*. Inner Truth Books.

Eckes, A., Großmann, N., & Wilde, M. (2018). Studies on the effects of structure in the context of autonomy-supportive or controlling teacher behavior on students' intrinsic motivation. *Learning and Individual Differences*, *62*, 69–78. https://doi.org/10.1016/j.lindif.2018.01.011

Engel, S. (2011). Children's need to know: Curiosity in schools. *Harvard Education Review*, *81*(4), 625–645. https://doi.org/10.17763/haer.81.4.h054131316473115

Engel, S. (2021, June 19). Curiosity. *Slate School Education Idea Lab Virtual Summit*. https://ms-my.facebook.com/SlateSchool/videos/education-idea-lab-virtual-summit-presents-susan-engel/513046766713371/

Engel, S., & Randall, K. (2009). How teachers respond to children's inquiry. *American Educational Research Journal*, *46*(1), 183–202. https://doi.org/10.3102/0002831208323274

Frazier, B. N., Gelman, S. A., & Wellman, H. M. (2009). Preschoolers' search for explanatory information within adult: child conversation. *Child Development*, *80*(6), 1592–1611. www.jstor.org/stable/25592097

Furlan, S., Agnoli, F., & Reyna, V. F. (2013). Children's competence or adults' incompetence: Different developmental trajectories in different tasks. *Developmental Psychology*, *49*(8), 1466–1480. https://doi.org/10.1037/a0030509

Grover, H. (2022, January 14). The beauty of wonder. *Slate School Blog*. https://slateschool.org/head-of-school-blog

Guilford, J. P. (1968). *Intelligence, creativity and their educational implications*. Robert Knapp.

Hobson, T. (2021, December 2). Teaching within the cracks. *Teacher Tom: Teaching and learning from preschoolers*. https://teachertomsblog.blogspot.com/2021/12/teaching-within-cracks.html

Hoff, E., Laursen, B., & Tardif, T. (2002). Socioeconomic status and parenting. In M. H. Bornstein (Ed.), *Handbook of parenting: Biology and ecology of parenting* (pp. 231–252). Lawrence Erlbaum Associates Publishers.

Kang, M., Hsu, M., Krajbich, I., Loewenstein, G., McClure, S. M., Wang, J., & Camerer, C. (2009). The wick in the candle of learning: Epistemic curiosity activates reward circuitry and enhances memory. *Psychological Science*, *20*, 963–73. https://doi.org/10.1111/j.1467-9280.2009.02402.x

Kelly, D. J., Quinn, P. C., Slater, A. M., Lee, K., Gibson, A., Smith, M., Ge, L., & Pascalis, O. (2005). Three-month-olds, but not newborns, prefer own-race faces. *Developmental Science*, *8*(6), F31–F36. https://doi.org/10.1111/j.1467-7687.2005.0434a.x

Komatsubara, T., Shiomi, M., Kanda, T., & Ishiguro, H. (2018). Can using pointing gestures encourage children to ask questions? *International Journal of Social Robotics*, *10*, 387–399. https://doi.org/10.1007/s12369-017-0444-5

Kurkul, K. E., & Corriveau, K. H. (2018). Question, explanation, follow-up: A mechanism for learning from others? *Child Development*, *89*(1), 280–294. https://doi.org/10.1111/cdev.12726

Lapidow, E., & Walker, C.M. (2020). Informative experimentation in intuitive science: Children select and learn from their own causal interventions. *Cognition*, *201*, 104315. https://doi.org/10.1016/j.cognition.2020.104315

Lloyd-Fox, S., Blasi, A., McCann, S., Rozhko, M., Katus, L., Mason, L., Austin, T., Moore, S. E., Elwell, C. E., & BRIGHT project team. (2019). Habituation and novelty detection fNIRS brain responses in 5- and 8-month-old infants: The Gambia and UK. *Developmental Science*, *22*(5), e12817. https://doi.org/10.1111/desc.12817

Lone, J. M., & Burroughs, M. D. (2016). *Philosophy in education*. Rowman & Littlefield.

Luo, J., Yuan, J., Qiu, J., Zhang, Q., Zhong, J., & Huai, Z. (2008). Neural correlates of the belief-bias effect in syllogistic reasoning: an event-related potential study. *Neuroreport*, *19*(10), 1073–1078. https://doi.org/10.1097/WNR.0b013e3283052fe1

Moore, S. G., & Bulbulian, K. N. (1976). The effects of contrasting styles of adult child interaction on children's curiosity. *Developmental Psychology*, *12*, 171–172. https://doi.org/10.1037/0012-1649.12.2.171

Post, T., & Walma van der Molen, J.H. (2018). Do children express curiosity at school? Exploring children's experiences of curiosity inside and outside the school context. *Learning, Culture and Social Interaction*, *18*, 60–71. https://doi.org/10.1016/j.lcsi.2018.03.005

Right Question Institute: A catalyst for microdemocracy. (n.d.). https://rightquestion.org/

Robinson, K. (2008). *Changing education paradigms* [video]. RSA: The Royal Society for the Encouragement of Arts, Manufactures and Commerce.

Robinson, K. H., Diaz, C. J., & Townley, C. (2020). Constructions of knowledge and childhood: Addressing current affairs with children with a focus on parents' practices and children's news media. *Contemporary Issues in Early Childhood*, *20*(4), 324–336. http://doi.org/10.1177/1463949119888483

Robinson, K. H., & Jones-Diaz, C. (2016). *Diversity and difference in childhood: Issues for theory and practice* (2nd ed.). Open University Press.

Schmidt, R., Armstrong, L., & Everett. T. (2007). Teacher resistance to critical conversation: Exploring why teachers avoid difficult topics in their classrooms. *The NERA Journal*, *43*(2), 49–55.

Sears, J. T. (2009). Interrogating the subject: Queering elementary education, 10 years on. *Sex Education*, *9*(2), 193–200. https://doi.org/10.1080/14681810902829653

Simard, S. W. (2018). Mycorrhizal networks facilitate tree communication, learning and memory. In F. Baluska, M. Gagliano & G. Witzany (Eds.), *Memory and learning in plants* (pp. 191–213). Springer.

Slater, A. (2004). Novelty, familiarity, and infant reasoning. *Infant and Child Development*, *13*, 353–355.

Sonu, D. (2020). Playing slavery in first grade: When "developmental appropriateness" goes awry in the progressive classroom. *Multicultural Perspectives*, *22*(2), 106–112. https://doi.org/10.1080/15210960.2020.1741369

Suzuki, S. (1973). *Zen mind, beginner's mind*. Weatherhill.

Walton, G. M., & Cohen, G. L. (2011). A brief social-belonging intervention improves academic and health outcomes of minority students. *Science*, *331*(6023), 1447–1451. http://doi.org/10.1126/science.1198364

Wolk, S. (2008). Joy in school. *Educational Leadership*, *66*(1), 8–15.

Zimmerman, B. (n.d.). The importance of encouraging our children to question. Retrieved from https://makebeliefscomix.com/learning-to-question/

4

Empowering Young Children for Autonomy and Agency
How to Nourish Freedom, Self-Determination and Confidence

Next to the right to life itself, the most fundamental of all human rights is the right to control our own thoughts and behaviors (Holt, 2004). Young children are rarely allowed this right, and even more rarely when they are at school. Ironically, the inventor of kindergarten in 1837, German philosopher and teacher Friedrich Wilhelm Fröebel, had two unwavering beliefs: that children should play whatever and however they want, and that their activities should be free from adult influence. Today most children are supervised and monitored, rewarded and punished, coerced and controlled throughout their school days, as a result of the external pressures on teachers to show that kids are learning in a predictable fashion, like a business needs to meet its bottom line. Our current education model is edging toward an industrial capitalism model, but that is not at all in concert with how children's minds and brains work. If the thrill of exploring new

DOI: 10.4324/9781003202875-5

ideas is replaced by anxiety, boredom and alienation, we have failed our children.

Empowering young children means giving them back at least some control over their own actions. Agency and autonomy allow kids to wonder about and explore and discover what it is they want to know. And learning is far and away the most effective for young kids when they voluntarily participate in it (Smith, 1998). Skilled educators know when to offer insights, questions or materials to boost a child's learning, but they also know when to get out of the way (Sobel, 2015). The key for deep learning is trust between the instructor and the learner. Then if the instructor says, "I think you need to do this," it is not a commend, it is not enforced, but the child will want to do it willingly, out of authentic respect. Giving advice as a wise elder is completely different from bossing around kids all day. Remember, when a child is genuinely interested and excited about something, he or she will activate completely different networks of the brain. Desire is a superhighway for learning. On the flip side, a child is unlikely to learn anything meaningful from an experience that others have bribed, threatened, bullied, wheedled or otherwise tricked them into doing (Sánchez Tyson, 2019). For the best learning in kids, parents and teachers should aim for the fewest external pressures possible. Let kids cultivate and pursue their own interests, and they will do it with passion!

Evolutionary and Developmental History of Autonomy and Agency

In order to give kids true agency, we also have to trust them. Well, we can certainly trust children when it comes to learning. Children are by far *the best* learners – they learn the most complex skills with ease and joy (and far more easily than adults with respect to many skills, as previously mentioned). Preschoolers, toddlers and even infants learn constantly and effortlessly. For example, starting from just a few months old, infants will manipulate and play with objects in the particular ways that will promote their learning. When they are in a busy or cluttered environment, infants will automatically shift their attention to the most "learnable" parts of the available surround (Gweon & Schulz, 2011). They do not need to be taught to do this, just as they need no instruction to learn to talk. In fact, up to their teenage years, kids learn and use new words at an average rate of 3,400 words per year. That's nearly ten new words every single day! Which kids learn the most words? (I will give you a hint: It is not the ones who most regularly ace their vocabulary tests). It is the ones who read the most. But of course, these kids aren't reading books in order to learn words. They are reading books because they enjoy them (Smith, 1998). Studies show across the board that children's learning is significantly deeper when they are given the opportunity to discover on their own before being given any instruction at all (Sobel & Sommerville, 2010).

The social facts of our education system have told us that for learning to be meaningful, it should be hard work. However, when we closely examine how children learn, we discover pretty quickly that the best learning – deep and lasting and useful – is not at all effortful to acquire. We humans are always learning, throughout our entire lives, often without even noticing and certainly without force or serious study. One example of this effortless learning is our cultural rules surrounding eye contact. We have learned that the length of time in which we politely hold the gaze of someone we are speaking to matters for social decorum. This amount of time varies between cultures, with the difference between a respectful gaze and a rude stare within a couple of milliseconds of each other. Learning the rules for eye contact was the byproduct of other implicit evolutionary goals of ours, like being accepted and loved by our social groups (Smith, 1998). Additional examples of effortless learning abound in the research: children in the slums of Delhi can learn to use computers without any instruction, just as children in the Congo basin can learn to learn large knives to whittle instruments out of wood (Hewlett et al., 2011; Mitra, 2003). The Mbya kids of Argentina learn innumerable skills by observing keenly and pitching into shared social endeavors. They do it on their own initiative – they want to participate because it matters for family, community, success and well-being (Remorini, 2015). In fact, being part of shared community endeavors is where and how all kids do their best learning. This is far more powerful than instruction.

How Autonomy Facilitates and Deepens Learning

When kids get to choose what they do, they become self-motivated, self-directed, responsible and independent. Dr. Emmi Pikler, an Austrian pediatrician who was famous for her respectful and egalitarian treatment of infants and children, opened and ran the famous Lóczy orphanage in Hungary during World War II for infants who had lost their parents to the war. Under her tutelage, caregivers at the orphanage did nothing "to" a baby or child – all caregiving was done "with" the little one instead. And all children in the orphanage were allowed to play and explore freely (Emmi Pikler Approach, n.d.). Pikler believed that babies, like seeds growing into plants, did not need any teaching to develop as nature intended; they would learn to walk, talk, self-soothe and interact appropriately, if only we could get out of their way (Levy, 2022). Our help and support, Pikler believed, may actually interfere with what the child is doing and thinking. But when we let children be uninterrupted, they have the chance to experience independence and mastery of their worlds. "Leave them alone to explore," was her mantra.

The developmental science research shows indisputably that when children are given autonomy, they learn more effectively and they learn more. Dozens of experimental studies have shown this effect. Autonomous kids report feeling better about themselves and they perform better in school (Zhou et al., 2009). In one experiment, students who completed science lessons based on their own interests and goals exhibited significantly higher focus, more active learning and greater lasting knowledge (Hofferber et al., 2014). In another study, hundreds of children reported on their learning experiences after each lesson, each day for one week. They simply commented on why they completed each task. The response options were things like: "I enjoyed it," "I chose to do it" and "I was interested in it" versus

"I had to do it" or "My teacher wanted me to do it." The children also reported on how hard they had worked and how confident they felt about what they had learned. Results were crystal clear. Students who engaged more deeply in the lessons were the ones who had been autonomous, choosing to do them out of interest and enjoyment (Malmberg & Martin, 2019).

Slate School organizes its curriculum around children's own goals and projects. Every Monday, each student decides what he or she has for a goal for the week, something that belongs entirely to them. (This practice is available to all teachers – it takes only minutes of a Monday circle time or community meeting.) A child's goal might be to get better at cartwheels, or to learn the nine times table math facts, or to beat their brother in chess. Whatever the goal, each child then decides on a commitment for the week to try to get there. ("Every time I play outside, I am going to do ten cartwheels" or "1 am going to review my math facts before bed each night" or "I'm going to play chess as many times as I can.") The children announce their commitment publicly to their class-room community, who will then say, "Awesome! We'll hold you to it!" At the end of the week, students check off whether they have stuck to their commitment, regardless of whether they have met their goal. Sometimes the commitments need adjusting for the next week, but the metacognitive gains and ownership of learning is strengthened regardless.

In the same spirit of agency, children at Slate School research, explore and carry out Personal Projects 5–6 times per year. Whether in kindergarten or in third grade, it is easy to tell when a child has landed their passions on a topic of deep interest – you can see it in their play, in class, at home. They talk about it during snack time and free time. They find links from their ideas to dozens of other areas of study, across vast interdisciplinary domains. And, of course, once kids are studying what they are authentically interested in, they will continue to delve deeper. A study on how birds coordinate and form the big Vs in the sky to migrate could morph into a study on the aerodynamics of flight or into the geography of South America, depending on the child, with an immense amount of learning in either case. The teacher becomes a helper in discovering genuine passions, scaffolding the information gathering and representing the process (J. Mountcastle, personal communication, January 26, 2022).

"But wait …" you might be thinking. "You just told me in Chapter 1 that kids need to collaborate and work together to best learn. If I give them autonomy, they will be only focused on themselves and their own desires." In fact, autonomous kids still thrive most by working together, they just feel fully in charge of their actions (and fully responsible for themselves) within collaborative groups. Autonomous kids are the opposite of self-centered because they can relax into the space without always feeling imposed upon. Anthropological research shows that respect for children's initiative is actually common in collaborative cultures, such as many indigenous communities (Rogoff, 2014). One recent study showed that Chinese children (within a very collectivist culture) achieved optimal classroom adaptation – as indexed by their interest and perceived competence in the topics – when they were given autonomy. Kids at the same school who were mostly told what to do by teachers had a more strained adjustment to their school experience (Zhou et al., 2009). Teachers who promote autonomy tend to offer their students choice and meaningful rationales for all learning activities, give them informative feedback without resorting to guilt or shame and allow them the space to decide for themselves how they want to learn (Hofferber et al., 2014). Research has shown again and again that autonomy-supportive environments boost students' learning across many cultures and contexts.

Why don't teachers do this more often? The major reason teachers use controlling, rather than autonomy-supportive strategies in the classroom is because they are being controlled themselves. The more that teachers are managed from above (the more they perceive pressure from imposed curriculum and toward meeting specific performance standards), the less likely they are to be autonomy supportive toward their students (Roth et al., 2007). But agency is not all or nothing. Teachers can find small and meaningful ways to subvert the external pressure on them to script their school days, and to open up opportunities for children's autonomy by sprinkling it throughout the curriculum. First-grade teacher at Ron Nunn Elementary School,

Mallory Muniz, has empowered her students in literacy by prioritizing their own stories. Rather than her choosing what to read aloud, Ms. Muniz's emerging readers write and share their original stories, both true and invented. It is no surprise that the children want to tell their own stories. After all, storytelling is a deep part of our human legacy and oral tradition. These children also desire to crystallize their storymaking experiences by writing them down in beautiful handmade books. When a child feels ready, Ms. Muniz staples their book together and they read their story aloud to the class. The other kids clap and ask questions that the reader/writer can answer. The students are so excited to make and read books that there is a long list of children waiting patiently to read aloud, like a mini-Moth Story gathering or a poetry slam. When they finish another lesson or assignment, they always ask, "Can I work on my book?" No coercion needed with read-alouds for this bunch.

Harms of Surveillance (and Even Praise)

When kids are watched and overseen, they become self-conscious, which inherently creates less agency and less autonomy. It doesn't take much for a child to be impacted by the adult gaze. Saying, "I love your drawing!" may get a child to keep drawing for as long as we keep watching and praising. But, warns Lilian Katz, one of the country's leading authorities on early childhood education, once the attention is withdrawn from the child, they will not touch the activity again (Kohn, 2001). A sizable and growing body of scientific research has shown that the more we reward kids for doing something, the more they tend to lose interest in whatever they had to do to get the reward. The point of the activity shifts, from drawing, thinking, creating or getting lost in the act to getting the praise, the sticker or the points on a chart. In a now classic study, young children who were frequently praised for displays of generosity tended to be *less* generous on an everyday basis than other children were. Every time they had heard "Good sharing!" or "I'm so proud of you for helping," they became a little less interested in sharing or helping for its own sake. Those actions came to be seen not as something valuable in their own right but as something they had to do to get that reaction again from an adult. Generosity became a means to an end (Rice & Grusec, 1975).

Building kids up with praise may be effective at getting them to behave as we want for a short while, but it is vastly different from empowering children to become thoughtful people who choose their actions and take responsibility for them. Praise works well for the short term because young children are longing for our approval. But beware of exploiting that hunger for our convenience. The more we say, "I like the way you drew that tree," the more kids come to rely on *our* evaluations, *our* judgments about what's good and bad, rather than learning to create their own values and judgments. "Good job!" is just as much an evaluation as "Bad job!" when it comes to letting the child know who is in power (Kohn, 2001).

Self-consciousness can also quash creativity. For example, if a young writer is afraid of the embarrassment of not knowing how to spell a word, they can easily get stuck on the minutiae of "How do I spell this word?" rather than focusing on, "What would I like to say to the world?" Lacking the confidence to spell words within their vocabulary is enough to halt the creative process or lead a child to choose a less sophisticated or less specific term (Schrodt et al., 2020). In fact, kids often report feeling that they can't yet write about things they love. But the technique of "brave spelling," when a child is empowered to boldly spell words as they sound, opens up creativity while also enhancing reading skills and phonological awareness (Ouellette & Sénéchal, 2017). Encouraging our young students to use their own unconventional spellings does not hinder the development of accurate spelling. Quite the contrary, in longitudinal studies, brave spelling strengthens the relationship between phonological understanding and proper spelling (Ouellette & Sénéchal, 2017). One class of 12 kindergartners who were taught brave spelling techniques, like "slowly stretch out the word like a turtle" or "write down as many sounds as you can hear," used 240 different words containing five or more letters. Brave spelling gave these children agency, allowing them to become independent and inspired writers and also increased their academic achievement (Schrodt et al., 2020).

Rather than positioning children's learning assessment as a judgment, it can be framed as an opportunity to develop skills of self-reflection. First-grade teacher Mallory Muniz uses metacognition as a form of agency when she assesses her first graders' learning. This gets them away from doing work merely to please her, the teacher, and also gets them away from the mindset of being judged. She has them reflect on why a skill is important for them, what it means to them. Then they ask themselves, "Am I learning this?" or "Can I do better than yesterday?" They show and tell her about their own learning at the end of a lesson: "I can practice blending short 'o' sounds in words, like mop, dog, got using a stretchy snake tool or a reading finger." Then they can determine where they are in their learning process, by turning their completed work in to the red basket, if they are still a bit unsure; the yellow basket if they're getting to where they want to be, but just need a bit more practice; the green basket, if they feel they have mastered a concept enough to teach one of their peers. This combines awareness with ownership of their learning process.

How Autonomy Nourishes Freedom, Self-Determination and Confidence

Kids need to know how to govern their own behavior in order to become self-determined, socially responsible and critically aware participants in their worlds. If we want education to be about social transformation, we must give learners opportunities for autonomy (Jiménez Raya et al., 2007). After all, if kids have never had the chance to make tough choices (or any choices at all), how will they get good at navigating complex and challenging decision making? How will they learn to solve conflicts or to stand up for something? Practicing bravery goes beyond spelling; it impacts kids' entire lives! Autonomy helps personal growth by enhancing self-knowledge, responsible self-agency, self-regulation and self-direction; it also helps with socioemotional growth by enhancing respect for others, negotiation, co-operation and interdependence. The goal of education should be to transform, rather than reproduce, the status quo.

Thus, we need to teach children democratic and emancipatory ideals (Parnell & Procter, 2011).

Placemaking as Autonomy

The physical environment of schools tend to be ordered and controlled by staff and are typically a manifestation of adults' power (Foucault, 1980). However, some schools are discovering just how empowering the act of placemaking can be for young children. A child owning the physical environment of the classroom is a significant challenge to the traditional power structures of a school. But it can invoke meaningful engagement and agency in children. In many Danish preschools, there is a designated space (sometimes an entire room) that is decorated and owned by children, with no adults allowed. This gives the kids a respite – someplace to go to just be with children, a space to regroup or just to feel free. Along the same lines, one primary school in Sheffield, England, allowed the students to make decisions on how to use their school space as part of an experiment in flexible and autonomous learning. The children decided to transform a corridor, which was once purely used for getting to other places, into a space for play. Before the re-purposing, the children described the hallway as "boring," "dull" and "cold." But after being allowed to design the space themselves, the children regularly made up games, told stories, jumped, ran and climbed there. This hallway was redefined as an exciting, imaginative, vibrant and fun part of their school. "Why don't we put some balls in there … for football?" asked one child. Placemaking, in this instance, encouraged the children's autonomy, a vision of education as empowerment and transformation rather than oppression and reproduction. These empowered learners became active rather than passive. Further, holding some power promoted a shared responsibility for ensuring everyone felt at ease to explore and create alongside one another. What is often called the most difficult conceptual and practical issue confronting society today – that is, developing inclusive, emancipatory communities – was achieved in this school by granting kids some modicum of autonomy (Parnell & Procter, 2011).

Sample Nourishment of Freedom, Self-Determination and Confidence

A powerful example of agency and autonomy promoting freedom, self-determination and confidence is the Japanese method of "mimamoru." Mimamoru is a blending of Japanese words *mi*, meaning watch and *mamoru*, meaning guard or protect. It's a non-intervention practice that involves letting even the youngest children autonomously handle their own disagreements. In early childhood, children must to learn to navigate among their peers, who may have competing interests and desires and who are likely coming from different power dynamics at home. Peer conflict can emerge suddenly and in unpredicted ways, from verbal exchanges to physical fights (Burdelski, 2020). Since conflict is an essential part of human relationships, learning how to engage in and resolve conflict is central to becoming a competent and ethical member of a social group.

Whereas most early childhood educators would immediately intervene in a fight between children, Japanese preschools have a more patient and hands-off approach that creates opportunities for children to autonomously learn interpersonal skills. In the mimamoru method, inappropriate behaviors, are not necessarily considered to be wrong or to require adults' intervention. These behaviors are rather viewed as social immaturity. Indeed, young children often become frustrated when they are unable to verbalize their feelings, and as a result they may engage in more physical fights (Kubo, 2011). But physical fights can also create important opportunities to teach children appropriate emotional and social skills, and to promote character development (Nakatsubo et al., 2021). When an adult steps in immediately to stop a conflict between children, they are not allowing those children the opportunity of learning about what is going on and how they should behave to manage it.

This does not mean that teachers using mimamoru ignore the safety of the children in their care. Far from it! Teachers will intervene anytime the risk of harm to a child becomes greater than the benefit for the involved children to learn. In fact, to be sure the children feel safe, teachers practicing mimamoru will usually move physically closer to the children involved in an altercation. They will be ultra-present and bear witness instead of getting involved. Although the mimamoru approach looks passive, it challenges educators to remain patient, to watch and wait for the children to think and act on their own. An underlying assumption of this Japanese practice is adults' trust in children's inherent goodness, more specifically, their ability to learn through everyday social interactions. Intentionally allowing children to handle their own disagreements in this way gives children the immediate visceral experience of "It hurts!" (physical pain) or the emotional feeling of, "Oh no, I shouldn't have done it!" (guilt).

This hands-off approach allows children to try on a variety of strategies for resolving their own disagreements, and also for mediating conflicts among others (Burdelski, 2020). Further, mimamoru develops the ability to take another's perspective. Peer conflict, after all, is an important catalyst for learning empathy and developing social skills. Japanese early childhood educators understand that children's cognitive, social and emotional skills can be developed autonomously, through their authentic interactions with peers, better than they can from adults' direct instruction and top-down approaches (Nakatsubo et al., 2021). Sometimes Japanese educators will even deliberately invoke mini-conflicts or scarcity in desired toys and materials in order to create social challenges for the children to learn to navigate (Nakatsubo et al., 2021).

When kids are socialized by other kids, the effect is more immediate and powerful than being told to do something by an adult. Take the following example: one morning, Ken and Takuya were arguing over a butterfly net. Ken refused to share the butterfly net with Takuya, who was crying. Their argument evolved into a physical fight. They hit each other and Takuya bit Ken's arm! Kumi, a 5-year-old who had emerged as a leader of this multi-age classroom, was observing the situation. Mr. Yoshida, the early childhood teacher present at the scene, said nothing, but put his hand on Ken's arm and tried to stop Takuya's biting. He did not, however, stop their physical fight. Rather, Mr.

Yoshida quietly stepped up closer and watched the children. When other children began to leave for the playground, Kumi, the 5-year-old leader, stayed with Ken and Takuya to help them make up. She said to Takuya, "Hey, say you are sorry. What's wrong?" Takuya replied, "Ken didn't let me use the butterfly net." Kumi responded, "But Takuya, you bit him, right? So, you must apologize. Got it? Ken also is bad because he didn't lend you the net, but you bit him, right? So, both of you should apologize. OK? Say, 'I'm sorry'." Takuya then said she was sorry. Then Kumi announced that Ken must say "Sorry," too. Ken said, "I'm sorry." After apologizing to each other, the three children walked together to the playground. The other children accepted all three kids into their new game without saying anything, and they began to play peacefully together.

Mimamori can also be very powerful for children with disabilities. This gentle and patient practice allows children negotiate their differences from typically developing peers by creating a safe environment in which they can handle minor conflicts with peers, such as teasing, and recover from them (Kayama & Haight, 2013; Kayama & Yamakawa, 2020). One teacher commented, "Immediately pulling [children in conflict] apart is overprotecting them." When educators intervene or force children to apologize, that apology often means nothing to either child, because it is not authentically from them. Mr. Yoshida explained that he wants his students to experience genuinely feeling badly after fighting with or hurting one another. The negative feeling can make them want to apologize voluntarily rather than issue a meaningless apology forced by uncomfortable adults.

In Sum

We must beware of taking away valuable learning opportunities from children, simply because of our adult urge for control. We could be denying children powerful experiences because of our desire for efficiency or cleanliness, order or ease. But when we model our own "comfort with discomfort," we teach kids courage. When we slow down and let them know we trust them, we show children that we are fearless ourselves. Instead of scripting, surveilling and judging, find moments to let kids be free. You will give them the opportunity to be confident, to take risks, to solve problems creatively and go deep into their learning. Free kids can handle complex social situations themselves because they have experience with agency and responsibility. When we trust kids, know that they are inherently virtuous people and inherently great learners, we can let their ethics emerge organically in social situations. Empowering young children with agency and autonomy opens them to the skills they will need in their lives. It will give them the boldness and tenacity to experience and confront injustice.

References

Burdelski, M. (2020). "Say can I borrow it": Teachers and children managing peer conflict in a Japanese preschool. *Linguistics and Education*, *59*, 100728. https://doi.org/10.1016/j.linged.2019.04.002

Foucault, M. (1980). Two lectures. In C. Gordon (Ed.), *Power/Knowledge: Selected interviews and other writings, 1972–1977* (pp. 78–108). Pantheon Books.

Gweon, H., & Schulz, L. (2011). 16-month-olds rationally infer causes of failed actions. *Science*, *332*, 1524. https://doi.org/10.1126/science.1204493

Hewlett, B. S., Fouts, H. N., Boyette, A. H., & Hewlett, B. L. (2011). Social learning among Congo Basin hunter-gatherers. *Philosophical Transactions B*, *366*(1567), 1168–1178.

Hofferber, N., Eckes, A., & Wilde, M. (2014). Effects of autonomy supportive vs. controlling teachers' behavior on students' achievements. *European Journal of Educational Research*, *3*(4), 177–184. https://doi.org/10.12973/eu-jer.3.4.177

Holt, J. (2004). *Instead of education: Ways to help people do things better*. Sentient Publications.

Jiménez Raya, M., Lamb, T., & Viera, F. (2007). *Pedagogy for autonomy in language education: Theory, practice and teacher education*. Authentik.

Kayama, M., & Haight, W. (2013). *Disability, culture, and development: A case study of Japanese children at school.* Oxford University Press.

Kayama, M., & Yamakawa, N. (2020). Acculturation, cultural self, and identity of Japanese children in U.S. schools: Insights from Japanese temporary resident and immigrant parents. *Identity, 20*, 1–20. https://doi.org/10.1080/15283488.2020.1782914

Kohn, A. (2001). Five reasons to stop saying "good job!" *Young Children, 56.*

Kubo, Y. (2011). The development of preschool children's conflict resolution with peers: Changes from four-year-olds to six-year-olds. *The Bulletin of the Faculty of Sociology Toyo University, 42*(2), 41–56.

Levy, A. (2022, January 17). Janet Lansbury's gospel of less anxious parenting. *The New Yorker.* www.newyorker.com/magazine/2022/01/17/janet-lansburys-gospel-of-less-anxious-parenting

Malmberg, L. E., & Martin, A. J. (2019). Processes of students' effort exertion, competence beliefs and motivation: Cyclic and dynamic effects of learning experiences within school days and school subjects. *Contemporary Educational Psychology, 58*, 299–309. https://doi.org/10.1016/j.cedpsych.2019.03.013

Maymon, Y., & Kaplan, H. (2007). Autonomous motivation for teaching: How self-determined teaching may lead to self-determined learning. *Journal of Educational Psychology, 99*, 761–774. https://doi.org/10.1037/0022-0663.99.4.761

Mitra, S. (2003). Minimally invasive education: A progress report on the "hole-in-the-wall" experiments. *British Journal of Educational Technology, 34*, 267–371.

Nakatsubo, F., Ueda, H., & Kayama, M. (2021). Why don't Japanese early childhood educators intervene in children's physical fights? Some characteristics of the *mimamoru* approach. *Early Childhood Education, 50*, 627–637. https://doi.org/10.1007/s10643-021-01184-3

Niemiec, C. P., & Ryan, R. M. (2009). Autonomy, competence, and relatedness in the classroom Applying self-determination theory to educational practice. *Theory and Research in Education, 7*, 133–144. https://doi.org/10.1177/1477878509104318

Ouellette, G., & Sénéchal, M. (2017). Invented spelling in kindergarten as a predictor of reading and spelling in grade 1: A new pathway to literacy, or just the same road, less known? *Developmental Psychology, 53*(1), 77–88. https://doi.org/10.1037/dev0000179

Parnell, R., & Procter, L. (2011). Flexibility and placemaking for autonomy in learning. *Educational & Child Psychology*, *28*(1), 77–88.

Pelletier, L. G., Se´guin-Le´vesque, C., & Legault, L. (2002). Pressure from above and pressure from below as determinants of teachers' motivation and teaching behavior. *Journal of Educational Psychology*, *94*, 186–196. https://doi.org/10.1037/0022-0663.94.1.186

Remorini, C. (2015). Learning to inhabit the forest: Autonomy and inter-dependence of lives from a Mbya-Guarani perspective. *Advances in Child Development and Behavior*, *49*, 273–288. https://doi.org/10.1016/bs.acdb.2015.09.003

Rice, M. E., & Grusec, J. E. (1975). Saying and doing: Effects on observer performance. *Journal of Personality and Social Psychology*, *32*(4), 584–593. https://doi.org/10.1037/0022-3514.32.4.584

Rogoff, B. (2014). Learning by observing and pitching in to family and community endeavors: An orientation. *Human Development*, *57*, 69–81. https://doi.org/10.1159/000356757

Sánchez Tyson, L. (2019). Trusting children: Lifelong learning and autonomy within the unschooling movement. *Journal of Unschooling and Alternative Learning*, *13*(25), 24–40.

Sénéchal, M. (2016). Testing a nested skills model of the relations among invented spelling, accurate spelling, and word reading, from kindergarten to grade 1. *Early Child Development and Care*, *187*(3/4), 358–370. https://doi.org/10.1080/03004430.2016.1205044

Schrodt, K., Fitzpatrick, E., & Elleman, A. (2020). Becoming brave spellers. *The Reading Teacher*, *74*(2), 208–214. https://doi.org/10.1002/trtr.1923

Smith, F. (1998). *The book of learning and forgetting*. Teachers College Press.

Sobel, D. M. (2015). Can you do it? How preschoolers judge whether others have learned. *Journal of Cognition and Development*, *16*(3), 492–508. https://doi.org/10.1080/15248372.2013.815621

Sobel, D. M., & Sommerville, J. A. (2010). The importance of discovery in children's causal learning from interventions. *Frontiers in Psychology*, *1*, 176. http://dx.doi.org/10.3389/fpsyg.2010.00176

The Emmi Pikler Approach: Compact ultimate guide. (n.d.). Ette Tete. https://ettetete.com/blogs/news/ultimate-article-about-emmi-pikler-apporach-and-principles?ls=en&cache=false

Zhou, M., Ma, W. J., & Deci, E. L. (2009). The importance of autonomy for rural Chinese children's motivation for learning. *Learning and Individual Differences*, *19*, 492–498. https://doi.org/10.1016/j.lindif.2009.05.003

5

Empowering Young Children to Take Their Time
How to Nourish Patience, Presence and Comfort with Discomfort

Every teacher wants their students to have transformative learning experiences. We hope for even our youngest learners that they can realize their place in the world, and their role in making it fair and just. But transformative learning moments are dynamic, non-linear and difficult to schedule in. They need openness and space to emerge. Changing our relationship to time is necessary for the best learning, and it also paves the road to active citizenship, social justice and ethics, by engendering presence of mind and patience. We must empower children by letting them control their own hours and days; by letting them slow down and become reflective; and by letting them learn how to reside in the present moment. If we want to grow children who become deep learners and engaged, ethical citizens, we need to let them learn how to manage their own time.

DOI: 10.4324/9781003202875-6

Evolutionary and Developmental History of Time in Childhood

Throughout human history, most children in the world have dwelled in free time, deciding how to spend their own hours, and they have mostly spent them playing with other children. This free time has been crucial to cognitive and brain development (Baron Nelson et al., 2019). Today, teachers, parents and caregivers often feel pressured to structure kids' free time in order to make it useful. They fear that if their children do not engage in enrichment activities, they will be left behind in our highly competitive society. Likewise, learning goals at school are so tightly formulated that every day feels crammed and hurried (Rantala & Määttä, 2012). As a result, many young children grow up without ever losing track of time, feeling free or choosing how to spend a day. It is so important for these well-meaning facilitators to know: the child development research shows that hyper-scheduling harms children (Veritas, 2018). While plans and schedules can make life more predictable at school and at home, tightly controlled timeframes thwart young children's need for autonomy and competence, disrupt their natural motivation, and ultimately impede their ability to learn (Van Der Kaap-Deeder et al., 2019). In other words, when we construct prescriptive schedules for kids, we rob them of experience with adaptive noticing and decision-making. Further, when being hurried, a young student has no time to enjoy learning, no opportunity to feel the great pleasure of hanging in there with a challenging task or solving a problem authentically over time.

What kids desire most of all is to be meaningful members of their ambient communities. As such, children are highly skilled at learning implicit values of the culture from their adults. If we adults model being "on the clock," constantly checking our messages, scheduling up every minute and fearing downtime, our children will learn anxiety. The idea that teachers are responsible for keeping kids busy is not present in the vast majority of cultures around the world, and definitely not throughout human history (Doucleff, 2021). Yet, somehow, we associate idle time at school with irresponsibility or, even worse, waste. Many teachers and students feel guilty if they are not constantly busy doing something (Kets de Vries, 2014). Instead, we need to practice being joyfully present with children. Kindergarteners in Japan regularly meditate in school, for up to an hour at a time. Their teachers model stillness and instruct them to "melt like ice cream" into their mats. When we show kids how to dwell in the present, they will begin to join us in our peaceful space and to notice for themselves what is important to engage in. This nourishes a kind of witnessing, an attention that we might describe as care for the present moment, attention to which makes an opening for itself (Skea & Fulford, 2021).

How Time Facilitates and Deepens Learning

When any activity is time-limited, even an interesting one, children explore less and learn less. Preschool teacher Anamaria Garcia has noticed that her students will delve much more deeply into art projects during after school care than they will during a daily 30-minute art block, even if the materials and opportunities are identical. She believes that the children can feel the time limitations and top-down nature of the regular school day, and so will not drop down into creativity. Italian pediatrician and pedagogue Maria Montessori observed the same: young children would keep their investigations on the surface if they felt that an interruption was imminent. On the other hand, when a child was allowed to work at his or her own pace, attention and engagement skyrocketed. Uninterrupted children, Montessori observed, "began to be completely transformed, to become calmer, more intelligent and more expansive" (1989, p. 21). In a recent research study, students were invited to explore trivia questions and answers on a tablet, receiving a fun fact with each click – things like: "Pablo Picasso was one of the suspects in the Mona Lisa robbery in 1911," or "A single blood cell takes around 60 seconds to pass through all the blood vessels in the human body." For some of the students, there was a "Stop" button on the bottom of their touchscreen and for others it was absent. When a "Stop" button existed, the participants soon pushed it; and as a result, they explored the facts far less. If there was no "Stop" button at all, yet the students could stop at any time, they both explored *and* remembered significantly more facts (Ben-Tov Sher et al., 2019). Feeling bound by time frames limits curiosity and, in turn, the deep engagement that underpins lasting learning.

It can be exhausting for children to switch gears, because shifting attention requires complex neurocognitive operations, including activation of the medial prefrontal, superior and inferior parietal, medial parietal and premotor cortices of the brain (Wager et al., 2004). When my son Alexei went to kindergarten he would just begin to focus on an activity, when inevitably it was always time for something else. "Clean up time!" or "snack time!" his teacher would enthusiastically call after 15 minutes. As a classroom volunteer, I could practically witness his little nervous system seize up with terror. Each transition was another wasted opportunity for genuine engagement. Deep learning cannot be scheduled into 15-minute spurts, and it might take some children several tries before they become captivated by an activity. Instead of switching gears for the whole group, a better strategy is to notice what individual children need. Mixing the pacing is a very effective and surprisingly underused pedagogical tool. We can let each child decide how much time they're going to spend on a particular activity or a task; we can empower them to make decisions about what is meaningful to them. Play theorist Tina Bruce encourages teachers to let kids joyfully try out and wallow in different scenarios throughout a given time period, to engage with different peers, moods, different chemistries of groups, events and circumstances. The concept of joyful wallowing connotes slowing down and immersing in things, or simply being – dwelling in a space – enabling more authentic attention with a lack of intention (Bruce, 2020).

The Faster Equals Better Myth

The best learning takes time: time to look closely and decide what is currently most important to ourselves. Young children learn best when they get authentically absorbed in something – be it a beetle, a puzzle or a puddle. But there is a creeping social myth that faster or sooner means smarter or better. I remember dreading my infant son's pediatrician appointments and neighborhood playground meetups, because he was a fascinating and non-linear "fits and starts" kind of learner. Questions like, "Is he rolling over yet?" or comments about a neighbor's baby being extra smart – already talking at 1½, already reading at 4, made me feel that I should be worried, or that I should be better structuring his time. But rather than rushing to collect competencies, children need time to exist in each unique developmental stage. Major cognitive leaps, like learning to speak or learning to read, emerge from the dynamic interplay of many factors – the most important of which is desire or motivation. Children gain an immense amount of new knowledge seemingly miraculously when they are in the sweet spot of maturation and hunger/ desire to learn.

There are no advantages to gaining specific skills or knowledge earlier than a child is ready. For example, learning to read at a younger age doesn't mean that a child will be a more voracious reader or a stronger reader at later ages. One key research study compared children who learned to read at age 5 with those who learned to read at age 7 and found no significant difference in reading skills between the two groups at age 12 (Suggate et al., 2013). Other research found that children taught to read before age 5 had more vision problems and more challenges reading than those taught to read at age 7 (Pica, 2015). Why, then, is having an early reader a badge of pride for parents or teachers? Or perhaps a better question is, why do those of us who have children who take less linear paths to developmental milestones feel as if somehow we have blown it?

Twentieth-century pediatrician Dr. Emmi Pikler advocated for children to learn at their own pace and schedule. She insisted that children in the Hungarian orphanage she ran were not rushed by other's expectations or compared with other children. Some might be prone to standing up at 7 months old, and some after 12 months, and both might be completely normal in their development. Some might skip walking and start by running. At the end of childhood, Pikler had faith that they would all come to the skills they needed (Emmi Pikler Approach, n.d.).

Sitting or walking earlier (or mastering other motor milestones sooner) does not at all predict future motor abilities or cognitive outcomes (Jenni et al., 2013). Likewise, children who start playing a particular sport, like baseball, when they are developmentally more mature regularly catch up to and even surpass those who started earlier (Pica, 2015).

Related research has shown that kids who moved more quickly through curriculum materials in school gained nothing over students who took longer with the same materials. In the same vein, the faster learners in one school subject were not consistently faster in other subjects. Nor were the faster learners at the beginning of the school year learning faster by the end of the school year (Hough, 2019). Another research team found that children with difficulties in number sense at the beginning of kindergarten were able to achieve appropriate, grade-level understanding by the end of kindergarten with zero interventions, simply with more time and experience in counting, number knowledge, number transformation, estimation and number patterns (Jordan et al., 2006). The enduring message here is that child development cannot be accelerated, and there is no reason to try to accelerate it. Childhood is not a dress rehearsal for adulthood. It is a separate, unique and very special phase of life.

Too Much, Too Soon in School

Why, then, are teachers being pressured to present particular skills and experiences at younger and younger ages, and to cram more and more content in their daily, weekly and yearly schedules? The last two decades have seen a staggering school curricula creep. Perhaps this is due to politicians' misunderstandings of cognitive development and how authentic learning happens. Policies like *No Child Left Behind* and *Race to the Top* mandated standardized tests, forcing young children to power through worksheets that prepare them for those tests (but that do nothing for deep and transformative learning). Public elementary magnet school principal Kurt Stanco discovered children who had not attended pre-K performed just as well in all kindergarten cognitive and socioemotional measures as those who had. "You have to ask yourself," he said, "why do we do pre-K?" (K. Stanco, personal communication, July 25, 2021). Teachers' personal perspectives have crept toward "more sooner," too. Whereas only 29 percent of U.S. public kindergarten teachers thought that kids needed to know the alphabet before kindergarten in 1998, by 2010, 62 percent thought so (Gallant, 2009). Suddenly, skills regarded as just barely reasonable for 5- and 6-year-olds, such as being able to sit at a desk and complete a worksheet using pencil and paper, were expected of much younger children lacking both the motor skills and the attention spans to be successful (Christakis, 2016). Early academics, our social facts of school tell us, will keep kids from "falling behind." However, the cognitive and developmental science research shows unequivocally that the opposite is true.

Dr. Arnold Gesell, a pediatrician and child development specialist in the early 20th century, spent countless hours observing children and noticed that every child went through predictable sequences and patterns of cognitive and learning milestones, each at his or her own pace. From 1925 to today, Gesell's developmental schedules have guided pediatricians and psychologists. The Gesell research center at Yale University has tested many thousands of children across schools and states and found that what kids can do at certain ages has remained relatively stable for close to a century. For example, most kids can draw a square by 4½ years old, but most cannot draw a triangle until 5½ (Pappano, 2010). How silly to try to skip certain steps of development in the name of productivity! The "earlier is better" mentality is not supported by neurological research, either. Formal academic instruction (which often amounts to passively receiving information) is never the way to optimize early brain development (Katz, 2015).

Unstructured Time for Learning

If we want to nourish deep learners, we need to let children decide how to spend at least some of their time. The ability to choose and negotiate how to spend one's own time, it turns out, is quite valuable for learning to make other decisions, switch gears and self-regulate in general. It makes sense, of course, that to become skilled at executive functions, children would need opportunities to practice them. Research has confirmed that executive functions in young children – the number one predictor of long-term academic achievement and success in school – are greatly enhanced in children who are allowed unstructured time (Barker et al., 2014; Nguyen & Duncan, 2019). In fact, kids who attend play-based preschool and kindergarten programs show superior learning outcomes to those who attend preschools and kindergartens with a more academic focus (Strauss, 2015). That is because non-linear and dynamic ways of spending time yield better results when it comes to deep learning. Kids truly need to spend time in that in-between space, to figure out how to handle problems, including the problem of how to spend time. Likewise, children need to practice endurance and patience in order to master other complex and social situations. Perseverance is a great skill for learning and for life. Many of our successes required persisting through some "unpleasure" – from struggling to sound out letters on the page when we were new readers, to waiting for spring seedlings to germinate when we started a garden (Duckworth et al., 2011). The ability to push through when confronted with obstacles has been linked to intelligence, school achievement and work success (White et al., 2017).

When we swap unstructured time for so-called learning achievement activities, we are in fact blocking children's optimal learning opportunity: the chance to encounter and negotiate complexity. In a recent study, bilingual preschoolers gained significantly more second-language skills from non-academic, unstructured, playful activities than from teacher-structured academic activities designed for literacy (Markova, 2017). Likewise, a study of 70 4- and 5-year-olds revealed that they learned more about the features of geometric shapes (a key aspect of school readiness) when they played with the shapes compared with when teachers gave them lessons about shapes. The kids who mucked around and played with the shapes were also more likely to remember the details a week later (Fisher et al., 2013).

Unstructured time also allows kids to work on their emotional development. In one study, in-depth interviews with more than 6,000 adults about their childhoods revealed a clear association between the amount of free time and free play individuals had as children, and their positive and adjustment and happiness as adults (Brown et al., 2011). In another research study, a group of children documented their foray back to unstructured time after years of being scheduled by others. Each child showed a similar pattern. At first, the children reported feeling helpless, and having no idea what to do with themselves. Part of the difficulty was that their parents had always recommended or set up activities for them, when they saw they were idle. Parents in the study confirmed this, indicating that they felt that they were not being "good parents" if their children not engaged in numerous activities. However, the study forced kids to transcend momentary discomfort and to manage their own time. They reported feeling significantly happier and also felt an increased sense of independence and self-reliance (Williams, 2006). Letting them manage their own time is one of the best gifts we can give children.

Neuroscience research has confirmed that the brain's prefrontal cortex is activated and strengthened when kids use complex cognitive maneuvers (like cognitive shifting and inhibitory control) in order to make their own decisions (Moriguchi & Hiraki, 2013; Smith et al., 2017). This is a call for us adults to be more patient with the unknowns of unstructured and unscheduled time, as opposed to organizing each moment. The messy and complex version of spending time is essential for the brain growth that underpins learning. Although the empirical data goes against our culture's bias that "quick equals smart," it is perfectly consistent with the fundamental developmental science principle of equifinality: there are many different developmental pathways to the same outcome (Gottlieb, 2003).

Pausing, Incubation and Problem Solving

Often when we are rushing children, it is because of our agendas, not theirs. At the root of these agendas is usually discomfort with downtime or fear of boredom. But even boredom can be a powerful experience for young children's learning. Transcending boredom (and being familiar with doing so) spikes creativity and unbounded thinking. In this way, it is a "lost art form" to be bored as a child, a precious and productive state. Boredom acts as a catalyst by pushing kids out of an unchallenging situation and into something else (Elpidorou, 2014). A recent research study found that people are significantly more creative after a boring activity. The participants in the study either just read, or read and copied down numbers from a phone book for 15 minutes. They were then tested on their creativity in a variety of ways, including completing divergent thinking tasks, like listing as many uses as they could come up with for a pair of paper cups, and other tasks like generating solutions to creative word problems. Those who did a boring task first were significantly more creative in the tasks that followed (Mann & Cadman, 2014). Boredom energizes us to locate change and variety. Busyness, on the other hand, does not allow for uninterrupted free associative thinking, creativity or insight (Belton & Priyadharshini, 2007). When we are bored, our thought processes might freely shift to other domains which can provide more stimulation. This is what we all know as daydreaming. Although daydreaming has a poor reputation as a classroom behavior, it can be crucial for planning and problem solving. When we daydream we gently percolate internal thoughts, remember and crystallize experiences and anticipate the future (Baird et al., 2011).

"Aha!" moments and solutions to problems can also pop unexpectedly to mind when we put an unsolved problem aside for a bit of time, giving insights an incubation period. Taking time away from the problem somehow allows a solution to emerge, even when no additional effort is added (Sio & Ormerod, 2009). Kids will focus and unfocus, leave and come back to projects and problems, if only they are allowed the time. In 1490, Michelangelo was commissioned to sculpt the figure of David for the Florence Cathedral. For nearly a year, he stared at the unfinished marble for hours on end day after day, doing nothing. When a friend saw him and asked the obvious question, "What are you doing?" Michelangelo replied, "Sto lavorando" ("I am working"). Years later the artist revealed that he needed to fully picture every muscle of David in the marble before beginning to work; only then could he set the figure free (Kets de Vries, 2014).

When children are pausing or disengaging or even zoning out, they are not "doing nothing." They may be considering several alternatives; they may be mulling a picture over in their mind's eye; they may be making associations, comparisons and contrasts. They may simply be clearing their heads. If we give children this time, their processing becomes richer, deeper and more abstract (Jennings, 2015). Studies indicate that longer pauses between teachers' questions and students' answers impact the depth, length, thoughtfulness and complexity of responses (Rowe, 1986). It should become an intentional part of our lessons to slow down and pause, as we can take this time to notice our body in space, the whole classroom, each student and the small details that surrounds us in the present moment. Pausing gives teachers a short break, too – a micro-vacation from the constant activity of a busy classroom (Jennings, 2015).

First-grade teacher Mallory Muniz does not have much opportunity to give her students free time. Their daily schedule includes many specialists and moving parts – including teachers offering outside services for children struggling with reading or math, ESL services and coordinated rotations in the computer lab or at the library. But Ms. Muniz still finds clever ways to include free time in the day. Each school day begins with a Good Morning song and then some downtime or play before starting to work. Kids can use Play-Doh, chat at their tables, take the chance to use math manipulatives as toys rather than tools and just transition into being together. Ms. Muniz will change her best laid plans when she notices that the kids are a bit tired after a transition, or when they really need to talk. She has tools to switch up the modality on a dime, like asking the kids to grab their clipboards and come to the rug with note paper. They lay on their bellies, talk to a partner and reset their inner attention and clocks. Being engaged is the number one priority, above and beyond a schedule. Collaborative free form time, even for a bit, even in a busy day, is time well spent.

Former United States poet laureate Billy Collins has called for a change in the tempo of education: "A shift from the urgencies and demands of the world to the more leisurely pace of discussion, the cadence of study and reflection, the seeming stop-time of engrossed thought." Collins believes that to truly learn, we need to pay attention not just to what is on the blackboard, but what is out the window. That bird. That cloud. He has said to young students, "Pay attention to your daydreams. Pay attention to what is on the periphery, for that is where the small wonders often reside" (Collins, 2003). One of the best modes for joyful and lasting learning is the "flow state," a mind frame hallmarked by its feeling of being outside of time. Flow is the holistic sensation that people have when they are completely engaged and immersed in an activity (Csikszentmihalyi, 1996). This feeling is described as intense concentration, time distortion and a feeling of being in control. Adults associate that state with the ultimate in pleasure – complete enjoyment and creativity – and among the best experiences in life. Some have reported that childhood itself (when unencumbered and un-imposed upon) was an exquisite and perpetual state of flow. What a gift!

How Time Nourishes Social Justice

Kids need to figure out how and when to slow down, to be comfortable with stillness, in order to develop into stewards of social justice. Slowness allows us to know what is happening, what is important – to check in with ourselves and to check in with others. Being present is a prerequisite for social justice work, because making ethical choices requires carefully taking in all of the relevant information. Children are set up to be engaged, caring and ethical citizens because they are perpetually in the present moment, rather than being preoccupied with the past or future, or with other agendas. Perhaps one reason that children are so good a being present is because everything is new – "rookies in life," as my potter friend Bob Brocken calls them. They are not operating on preconceived notions of how things ought to look or be, giving them an unusual open-mindedness. Moreover, children have fewer stories associated with the labels and the objects they are looking at. They are free to perceive the milieu with the freshness such that each moment is the first (Gowmon, 2018).

Slow Movements represent a political stance in response to our consumer capitalist efficiency model of living. Proponents of the Slow Food Movement in Italy have paved the way for Slow Education, claiming that we lose much when we are in a hurry all the time. A central idea shared by all Slow Movements is a desire to take more ownership over time. Going "Slow" in school is not about doing less; rather, it is about occupying and controlling time differently. If we can prioritize attentiveness, deliberation, thoughtfulness, open-ended inquiry, receptive attitudes, care and creativity, we can concoct space for meaningfulness and for genuine inquiry. Thus, the emphasis of the Slow Education Movement is on quality rather than quantity. Slowing down reflects a more ethical orientation toward the world: calm, still, patient, intuitive, reflective – about making real and meaningful connections with one another. Slowness in school entails using our time in ways that we deem worthwhile and meaningful, and not simply responding to perceived external pressures with little authentic meaning, like standardized tests (Hytten, 2017). Slow teaching has a strong social justice element and is concerned with making a difference in the whole lives of students (Leibowitz & Bozalek, 2018).

Teachers are often afraid to slow down, much in the same way that parents are afraid. Afraid to blow it. I remember when my babies graduated into eating solid food after nursing, and I suddenly felt such an immense responsibility to get them all of the nutrients they needed. When it was just milk, we had our bases naturally covered. But suddenly, I was trying to cram in enough calcium and protein and vitamins, and when my little toddlers would sometimes refuse to eat anything at all, I was panicked. My pediatrician told me something that was a game-changer for me. She said to focus on getting the right amount of nutrients into each child in a week, not in a day. This simple shift allowed me to loosen the time frame, and suddenly everything fell into place. It was completely doable to account for enough protein over the course of a week. Many teachers are in a similar panic, trying to make sure that kids are hitting these healthy marks for learning. If they can let down on the schedule a bit, look at learning over different lengths of time, that fluidity would make all of the difference. Let young children get enough reading and science and math over the course of a week, but if they want to spend all afternoon one day playing in a puddle, know that that is just as meaningful.

One of the silver linings of the Covid-19 global pandemic was that it gave families a chance to slow down. Parents who barely had time to grab a bagel while dashing out the door were suddenly able to sit down for heart-to-heart talks over homemade sourdough avocado toast (Reif, 2020). There were new puppies to be walked, stories to be read and backyard swings to be swung. Somers, New York Board of Education president Dr. Lindsay Portnoy and her partner, Gary, both busy professionals, expressed their gratitude at finally being able to do simple things with their two sons, ages 9 and 11. Dr. Portnoy commented, "We are being very mindful of this opportunity to spend time together. The other day, my oldest and I played on our tire swing for like 20 minutes. It was ridiculously fun" (Reif, 2020). As we move into our post-pandemic lives, it is the right moment to ditch linear notions of learning, and no longer allow efficiency to dominate and colonize our education system.

Patience and the willingness to wait peacefully help individuals make optimal decisions in their daily lives. When we develop the ability to be comfortable with discomfort – our own and that of others – we are more likely to challenge linear and hierarchical thinking. The Chinese word for patience is *nai-sin*, which holds the capacity for tolerance as a character trait. Arabic has two related words to cover these virtues: *sabr* and *tahammul*. The first denotes the capacity to accept adversity with calm and the latter denotes the capacity to carry on with dignity during states of suffering (Akhtar, 2015). Dating back to the 3rd or 4th century, in the Latin textbook of wisdom and morality known as The Cato, there is a line that reads, "Of human virtues, patience is most great." Similarly, the authors and negotiators of the Good Friday Peace Accords, which ended a period of horrific violence in Northern Ireland, noted that most of their job was about patience. Sometimes they had to wait out the obstructionists, but mostly they needed to patiently listen to everyone, to many sides and perspectives of the conflict. Once we master the discomfort of stillness, we can do anything.

We want to teach children the courage to wait, and by doing so, we will teach them to de-escalate aggression and its accompanying pain. Aggression can have a seductive quality to it – it can pull us in the direction of wanting quick relief or resolution. We strike out when we feel restless, agitated or ill at ease. If kids can learn to slow down that moment, just pause instead of immediately acting out, they can learn to find peace in themselves, their social groups and the world. Joy and happiness come from sitting still with the moodiness of energy until it rises, swells and passes by. When a painful situation inevitably occurs, children can learn to be patient (Chodron, 2006).

Sample Nourishment of Patience, Presence and Comfort with Discomfort

One of the best methods of nourishing patience in children is gardening! Gardening has many benefits for young children. They get to practice responsibility, love of nature, self-confidence, cooperation, good nutrition, creative design and problem solving. Garden experiences help young children understand plant and animal life cycles, soil and water conservation, weather, insects and wildlife. But perhaps the greatest of all skills gardens grow is patience. Gardening lets kids know in a visceral way that good things come to those who wait (Luna, 2020).

School gardens are not new. They were cultivated in Europe as early as the 19th century, and the first school garden was documented in the United States in 1891, in Massachusetts. But over the last 20 years, school gardening has become a global movement, and not just in places with land to spare. Take Taiwan, for instance. Most people in Taiwan live in urban apartment buildings without yards or outdoor space, so when Taiwanese children set out to make a school garden, odds are that they have never grown anything in that way before. But school gardening is blossoming in Taiwan as elsewhere, and the benefits for children are profound (Chang et al., 2016).

The art of patience in the garden begins with adults, and young children will follow your lead. The key is to not take shortcuts or shy away from things that take time. Weeds are an example. You will see weeds started by wind-blown seeds or deposited by birds. They can be frustrating to gardeners because they never completely go away. But for young children, weeds are fun to spot and identify. Dandelion, oxalis, clover, nutsedge and thistle pop up quickly and add an excitement to the process of upkeep. The vegetables and flowers you intend to grow will be much more slow-going (though seasoned school gardeners do recommend starting with somewhat quicker growing species for young children). Corn, pumpkins and sunflowers progress at a satisfying pace while still building patience. Set up each child with a log for recording plant growth on a daily or weekly basis. Seeing each plant grow and making note of its progress helps the kids learn to understand what is happening before them. Choose plants that appeal to all their senses: smell (sweet peas, lavender, mint, lemongrass and jasmine), taste (carrots, cherry tomatoes, strawberries, peas), touch (aloe vera, cacti, woolly lamb's ear, bottlebrush), color (marigolds, daffodils, petunias, snapdragons) and sound (high grasses to rustle in the wind). Slow down daily to notice the sensory gifts of each plant.

Wildflower gardens inspire patience in particular. Seedlings can be started in pots. At planting time, you need to consider the mature size of each plant and allow space between them to grow. Already, children will need to think of time in a different way. Dig planting holes twice as wide as the root ball, and plant at the same depth as they were growing in their pots. Always water thoroughly after planting and one or two times a week, (depending on rainfall), applying ½ inch of water at a time. Keeping empty cans placed in the garden while watering can help determine this amount. Use a ruler with the children to check water levels. Some wildflowers are annuals living only one season. These plants will reappear in your garden if you let their seeds naturally ripen and fall to open ground. Most wildflowers, however, are perennials and will live three to five years or longer. After wildflowers seeds have been dispersed, the old stems can be removed by cutting at the base. Remind the children that although the garden may look dead in winter, there may be eggs and larva of beneficial insects in its debris. Many roots will survive through the winter and produce sprouts next season (Seedlings for Schools Grant Program, n.d.). Be patient and let the kids learn to love the garden in all its natural seasons.

At Slate School in North Haven, Connecticut, the garden curriculum is integrated across the curriculum and incorporates children's own interests. The children choose what they will grow and then make garden plans – using both mathematical and spatial reasoning. This is a laborious process and takes a big investment of time. The kids ask and answer questions like "How many beans can we plant?" and in their planning, they learn the backstory of each vegetable's cultivation and use in human cultures. Once the plants begin to grow, their questions grow, too: "If I plant this tree branch, will it come back to life?" or "Why are these tomatoes a different shape or color than others?" Facilitators record these questions and turn them into further study. Children slowly and carefully document their observations in nature journals and as they make discoveries, those too lead to further ideas they can plan and carry out (Kenny, 2020).

In Sum

Optimal development is not in the service of end products but requires enough time in each developmental stage, accepting and allowing for uncertainty along the path, and being at peace with the process before knowing the outcomes. Complete absorption by young children is *the number one* foundation of transform-ational learning, and yet it cannot be scheduled in. We need to slow down and be present for that magic to emerge. Wondering and wandering, not efficiency, are what lead children to be transformed by their learning experiences.

References

Akhtar, S. (2015). Patience. *Psychoanalytic Review, 102*(1), 93–122. https://doi.org/10.1521/prev.2015.102.1.93

Baird, B., Smallwood, S., & Schooler, J. W. (2011). Back to the future: Autobiographical planning and the functionality of mind-wandering. *Consciousness and Cognition*, *20*, 1604–1611. https://doi.org/10.1016/j.concog.2011.08.007

Barker, J. E., Semenov, A. D., Michaelson, L. Provan, L. S., Snyder, H. R., & Munakata, Y. (2014). Less-structured time in children's daily lives predicts self-directed executive functioning. *Frontiers in Psychology | Developmental Psychology*, *5*(593), 1–16. https://doi.org/10.3389/fpsyg.2014.00593

Baron Nelson, M., O'Neil, S. H., Wisnowski, J. L., Hart, D., Sawardekar, S., Rauh, V., Perera, F., Andrews, H. F., Hoepner, L. A., Garcia, W., Algermissen, M., Bansal, R., & Peterson, B. S. (2019). Maturation of brain microstructure and metabolism associates with increased capacity for self-regulation during the transition from childhood to adolescence. *The Journal of Neuroscience: The Official Journal of the Society for Neuroscience*, *39*(42), 8362–8375. https://doi.org/10.1523/JNEUROSCI.2422-18.2019

Belton, T., & Priyadharshini, E. (2007). Boredom and schooling: A cross-disciplinary exploration. *Cambridge Journal of Education*, *37*(4), 579–595. https://doi.org/10.1080/03057640701706227

Ben-Tov Sher, K., Levi-Keren, M., & Gordon, G. (2019). Priming, enabling and assessment of curiosity. *Education Technology Research & Development*, *67*, 931–952. https://doi.org/10.1007/s11423-019-09665-4

Brown, S. L., Nobiling, B. D., Teufel, J., & Birch, D. A. (2011) Are kids too busy? Early adolescents' perceptions of discretionary activities, overscheduling, and stress. *Journal of School Health*, *81*(9), 574–580. https://doi.org/10.1111/j.1746-1561.2011.00629.x

Bruce, T. (2020). *Educating young children: A lifetime journey into a Froebelian approach. The selected works of Tina Bruce*. Routledge.

Chang, Y., Su, W., Tang, I., & Chang, C. (2016). Exploring the benefits of school gardening for children in Taiwan and identifying the factors influencing these benefits. *HortTechnology hortte*, *26*(6), 783–792. https://doi.org/10.21273/HORTTECH03074-16

Chodron, P. (2006). *Practicing peace*. Shambhala Publications.

Christakis, E. (2016). How the new preschool is crushing kids. *Atlantic*, *317*(1), 17–20.

Collins, B. (2003, Summer). On slowing down. *National Association of Independent Schools*. www.nais.org/magazine/independent-school/summer-2003/on-slowing-down/

Csikszentmihalyi, M. (1996). *Creativity: Flow and the psychology of discovery and invention*. HarperCollins Publishers.

Doucleff, M. (2021). *Hunt, gather, parent: What ancient cultures can teach us about the lost art of raising happy, helpful little humans*. Simon & Schuster.

Duckworth, A., Kirby, T., Tsukayama, E., Berstein, H., & Ericsson, K. (2011). Deliberate practice spells success: Why grittier competitors triumph at the national spelling bee. *Social Psychological and Personality Science*, *2*, 174–181. https://doi.org/10.1177/194855061 0385872

Elpidorou, A. (2014). The bright side of boredom. *Frontiers of Psychology*, *5*, 1–4. https://doi.org/10.3389/fpsyg.2014.01245

Fisher, K. R., Hirsh Pasek, K., Newcombe, N., & Golinkoff, R. M. (2013). Taking shape: Supporting preschoolers' acquisition of geometric knowledge through guided play. *Child Development*, *84*(6), 1872–1878. https://doi.org.sonoma.idm.oclc.org/10.1111/cdev.12091

Gallant, P. A. (2009). Kindergarten teachers speak out: "Too much, too soon, too fast." *Reading Horizons: A Journal of Literacy and Language Arts*, *49*(3). https://scholarworks.wmich.edu/reading_horizons/vol49/iss3/3

Gowmon, V. (2018). 6 ways children live in the present moment. *Healing for a New World*. www.vincegowmon.com/6-ways-children-live-in-the-present-moment/

Gottlieb, G. (2003). Probabilistic epigenesis of development. In J. Valsiner & K. J. Connelly (Eds.), *Handbook of developmental psychology* (pp. 3–17). Sage.

Hough, L. (2019). No need for speed: Study shows that faster isn't necessarily better when it comes to learning. Harvard Education Magazine. www.gse.harvard.edu/news/ed/19/08/no-need-speed

Hytten, K. (2017, March). Democracy and education in the United States. Oxford Research Encyclopedia of Education. https://doi.org/10.1093/acrefore/9780190264093.013.2

Jenni, O. G., Chaouch, A., Caflisch, J., & Rousson, V. (2013). Infant motor milestones: Poor predictive value for outcome of healthy children. *Acta Paediatrica*, *102*(4): e181. https://doi.org/10.1111/apa.12129

Jennings, P. A. (2015). *Mindfulness for teachers: Simple skills for peace and productivity in the classroom*. The Norton Series on the Social Neuroscience of Education. W.W. Norton & Company.

Jordan, N. C., Kaplan, D., Olah, L. N., & Locuniak, M. N. (2006). Number sense growth in kindergarten: A longitudinal investigation of children at risk for mathematics difficulties. *Child Development*, *77*(1), 153–175. https://doi.org/10.1111/j.1467-8624.2006.00862.x

Katz, L. G. (2015). *Lively minds: Distinctions between academic versus intellectual goals for young children*. Defending the Early Years.

Kenny, G. (2020, June 7). *The learners garden at Slate School: Described by environmentalist Grace Kenny*. https://youtu.be/A83NXjwBtQc

Kets de Vries, M. (2014). Doing nothing and nothing to do: The hidden value of empty time and boredom. *SSRN Electronic Journal*, *44*, 10. https://doi.org/10.2139/ssrn.2432964

Leibowitz, B., & Bozalek, V. (2018). Towards a Slow scholarship of teaching and learning in the South. *Teaching in Higher Education*, *23*. https://doi.org/10.1080/13562517.2018.1452730

Luna, C. (2020). Teaching kids the art of patience through gardening. *Tutor Doctor: How Learning Hits Home*. www.tutordoctor.com/blog/2020/february/teaching-kids-the-art-of-patience-through-garden/

Mann, S., & Cadman, R. (2014). Does being bored make us more creative? *Creativity Research Journal*, *26*(2), 165–173. https://doi.org/10.1080/10400419.2014.901073

Markova, I. (2017). Effects of academic and non-academic instructional approaches on preschool English language learners' classroom engagement and English language development. *Journal of Early Childhood Research*, *15*(4), 339–358. https://doi.org/10.1177/1476718X15609390

Merrell, K. W., & Gimpel, G. (2014). *Social skills of children and adolescents: Conceptualization, assessment, treatment*. Psychology Press.

Montessori, M. (1989). *To educate the human potential*. Clio Press.

Moriguchi, Y., & Hiraki, K. (2013). Prefrontal cortex and executive function in young children: a review of NIRS studies. *Frontiers in Human Neuroscience*, *7*, 867. https://doi.org/10.3389/fnhum.2013.00867

Nguyen, T., & Duncan, G.J. (2019). Kindergarten components of executive function and third grade achievement: A national study, *Early Childhood Research Quarterly*, *46*, 49–61. https://doi.org/10.1016/j.ecresq.2018.05.006

Pappano, L. (2010). Kids haven't changed: Kindergarten has new data support a return to "balance" in kindergarten. *Harvard Education*

Letter, *26*(5). https://laurapappano.com/wp-content/uploads/KIdsHaventChangedKhas.pdf

Pica, R. (2015). *What If everybody understood child development? Straight talk about bettering education and children's lives*. Corwin Press.

Rantala, T., & Määttä, K. (2012). Ten theses of the joy of learning at primary schools. *Early Child Development and Care*, *182*(1), 87–105. https://doi.org/10.1080/03004430.2010.545124

Reif, C. (2020, April 2). Families slow down as distance learning ramps up. TapInto. www.tapinto.net/towns/yorktown/sections/community/articles/families-slow-down-as-distance-learning-ramps-up

Rowe, M. B. (1986). Wait time: Slowing down may be a way of speeding up! *Journal of Teacher Education*, *37*, 43–50. https://doi.org/10.1177/002248718603700110

Seedlings for Schools Grant Program: Introduction to Wildflower Gardening. (n.d.). www.flawildflowers.org/wp-content/resources/pdfs/Publications/SFS_PlanningSchoolGarden.pdf

Sio, U. N., & Ormerod, T. C. (2009). Does incubation enhance problem solving? A meta-analytic review. *Psychological Bulletin*, *135*, 94–120. https://doi.org/10.1037/a0014212

Skea, C., & Fulford, A. (2021). Releasing education into the wild: An education in, and of, the outdoors. *Ethics and Education*, *16*(1), 74–90. https://doi.org/10.1080/17449642.2020.1822612

Smith, E., Anderson, A., Thurm, A., Shaw, P., Maeda, M., Chowdhry, F., Chernomordik, V., & Gandjbakhche, A. (2017). Prefrontal activation during executive tasks emerges over early childhood: Evidence from functional near infrared spectroscopy. *Developmental Neuropsychology*, *42*(4), 253–264. https://doi.org/10.1080/87565641.2017.1318391

Strauss, V. (2015, September 1). The decline of play in preschoolers – and the rise in sensory issues. *Washington Post*. www.washingtonpost.com/news/answer-sheet/wp/2015/09/01/the-decline-of-play-in-preschoolers-and-the-rise-in-sensory-issues/

Suggate, S. P., Schaughency, E. A., & Reese, E. (2013). Children who learn to read later catch up to children who learn to read early. *Early Childhood Research Quarterly*, *23*, 33–48. https://doi.org/10.1016/j.ecresq.2012.04.004

The Emmi Pikler Approach: Compact ultimate guide. (n.d.). Ette Tete. https://ettetete.com/blogs/news/ultimate-article-about-emmi-pikler-apporach-and-principles?ls=en&cache=false

Van Der Kaap-Deeder, J., Soenens, B., Mabbe, E., Dieleman, L., Mouratidis, A., Campbell, R., & Vansteenkiste, M. (2019). From daily need experiences to autonomy-supportive and psychologically controlling parenting via psychological availability and stress, *Parenting: Science and Practice*, *19*, 1–26. https://doi.org/10.1080/15295 192.2019.1615791

Veritas, D. (2018, January 29). *3 ways over-scheduling can hurt your kids*. American College of Pediatricians. https://archive.acpeds.org/3-ways-over-scheduling-can-hurt-your-kids

Wager, T. D., Jonides, J., & Reading, S. (2004). Neuroimaging studies of shifting attention: a meta-analysis. *NeuroImage*, *22*, 1679–1693. https://doi.org/10.1016/j.neuroimage.2004.03.052

White, R. E., Prager, E. O., Schaefer, C., Kross, E., Duckworth, A. L., & Carlson, S. M. (2017). The "Batman effect": Improving perseverance in young children. *Child Development*, *88*(5), 1563–1571. https://doi.org/10.1111/cdev.12695

Williams, J. D. (2006) Why kids need to be bored: A case study of self-reflection and academic performance. *RMLE Online*, *29*(5), 1–17. https://doi.org/10.1080/19404476.2006.11462028

6

Empowering Young Children for Dynamic Movement in Nature
How to Nourish Embodiment and Ecological Attunement

Kids are on the move, and their coming to knowledge is a full-body endeavor. Young children engage and learn through doing, and all of their sensory and perceptual systems take in information and respond to it, expressing multimodally what they have found. Sadly, moving around is increasingly rare in early-childhood classrooms, which are becoming more and more academic and structured, drawing an artificial line between "work time" and "playtime" and restricting kids physically (Dotson-Renta, 2016). Of course, during the tens of thousands of years of our human evolution, healthy, growing children would have spent much of everyday outside, running around with other kids in a sensory milieu that included dynamic emotional interactions and almost constant real-time problems to solve. We need to create scenarios for embodied and place-based learning to happen freely and collectively in order to generate creative, innovative, self-determining, interdependent and community-minded individuals (Marin, 2020).

DOI: 10.4324/9781003202875-7

Evolutionary and Developmental History of Moving, Embodied Learning

Ever wonder why taking a few running steps in the outfield helps you catch a fly ball? Or why you always feel better after a brisk walk? The way we move our bodies impacts the functioning of our brains and changes the nature of our thoughts (Jabr, 2014). Movement is a prerequisite for perception, attention and self-regulation. Moving allows the brain to perceive fine-tuned stimulation dynamically; to orient the sensory systems; to regulate attention and arousal. Young children devote most of their waking hours to movement. Running, jumping, wrestling and climbing are what it should mean to be a kid. Children's bodies, metabolisms and bone structures are designed to be active all day (Imus, 2008). Rather than trying to get children to stop fidgeting, we should embrace their tendency to move as a prerequisite for their growth and development.

How Movement Facilitates Deep Learning

In the course of a day, we all go through many different states of arousal. Sometimes we are "up," with hearts pounding; other times we're calm and our breathing is steady. When we're excited or upset, it is very difficult to concentrate. Adults have mostly learned how to regulate their arousal states – to bring the nervous system back down when it's too revved up and gear up when energy is low. We may walk around a bit, splash water in our faces or get a drink. We may take some deep breaths or step outside. Children need to learn such strategies. Telling them to sit still is not the best pedagogical model and generally won't help them change their state.

We should not aspire for still, quiet little bodies during young children's learning. Attention is first and foremost an active process (Ostroff, 2014; Parnell & Procter, 2011). Humans evolved our complex brains within a dynamic surround. For 99 percent of the time humans have lived on earth, we've been outside hunting for food, avoiding predators and moving from place to place. We needed to pay attention to survive. Consequently, our brains have been set up to operate best in changing environments (Gray, 2013; Medina, 2012). Self-regulation is a precursor to attention and uses the same brain systems (Rueda et al., 2004). Students who self-regulate well tend to focus their attention easily and, as a result, succeed at school. Because children develop foundational skills for self-regulation in the first five years of life (Galinsky, 2010), early childhood teachers play an important role in helping kids learn to regulate thinking and behavior. Preschool director Kiera Durett teaches children "belly breathing" by putting a beanbag on kids' stomachs and having them watch it rise and fall. Her students then belly breathe when they need to refocus on their bodies. Recess is of the utmost importance for self-regulation. For children to take care of their emotional and physical states and subsequently refocus, they must have enough time to take breaks and move freely. Research clearly shows that the longer the stretch of time children are confined to the classroom, the less attentive they become. After children play outside, their attention drastically improves (Pellegrini et al., 1995).

Teaching for Embodied Cognition

The more the whole body is involved in any learning experience, the more engrossed and focused the learner will be. Movement gives a child's brain a chance to "do" the information that they are learning, rather than to only see or hear it. It gives the mind information through more senses. Reaching, jumping and balancing teach children how to understand and negotiate their worlds. Also, physical movement couples nicely with other dimensions of sensation – visual, auditory or tactile – and being physical keeps students interested because they have to be engaged to keep up, literally, with their marching or dancing neighbors. The diverse brain regions activated when someone performs a movement while learning a concept will become linked together via neuronal networks. The more complex those networks are, the easier it will be to remember that concept later. This corresponds to indigenous ways of knowing, which are typically based on using the entire body in direct participation with the natural world (Cajete & Bear, 2000).

Physically active lessons can seamlessly combine movement with academics, with powerful effects. In one study, children learning the properties of centripetal force were divided into groups with a high-embodiment learning situation (where they swung objects overhead) and a low-embodiment learning situation, where they clicked a mouse to spin a virtual object. The kids who used their bodies showed significantly deeper understanding of the concepts a week later (Johnson-Glenberg et al., 2016). In a related study, two classes of first-graders wore an accelerometer for four weeks to measure their physical activity. One group attended their physical education classes and their math lessons separately. The other group learned the same math concepts, but in an integrated physical education and math lesson. Those who participated in the physically active math lessons had significantly higher scores in subtraction learning than their counterparts. But, more than that, the kids who learned math in an embodied way spent more time being physically active during a later free choice period (Cecchini & Carriedo, 2020). This could be due to motivation, or it could be due to cardiovascular exercise's impact on blood flow in the brain. Or perhaps these kids just got in the mode of spending their day moving and learning together.

In a program called Moved by Reading, scholars found that when students manipulated toys as they read, they remembered significantly more about the stories, and their comprehension was better than students who merely read the text. Despite the traditional view of learning as strictly mental, evidence like this suggests that the sensorimotor systems are integrated with learning at many levels (Glenberg, 2011). Similarly, researchers have discovered that forming angles with one's arms impacted children's understanding of and memory for different types of angles (Smith et al., 2014).

Elementary school teacher Paige Schulte uses movement activities and games when teaching geography skills. As a first-year teacher, she realized quickly that the methods for learning social studies (reading, writing and worksheets) were not working well with her students. She was as bored and frustrated as they were! Schulte's initial attempts in using movement simply involved the students rotating, revolving and using their arms to remember the difference between horizontal and vertical. She knew the approach was starting to work when she saw her students simulating the movements at their desks during a test (Schulte, 2005). We can recruit attention through movement in virtually any classroom lesson. Kinesthetic experiences expand children's creativity and understanding of their own bodies. Have students race around on scooters to match words with their definitions, which are printed on cards around the gym (Viadero, 2008). Let students show the answers to arithmetic problems by jumping the correct number of times. As choreographer and science educator Susan Griss (1994) points out, toddlers rolled down hills, flailed their arms and jumped for joy long before they began to express themselves with language. In a science lesson on sound waves, Griss has students guess the medium through which sound moves the fastest – air, water, or a solid. She lines students up in "molecule formations" (with the kids closest together representing molecules of a solid and those farthest apart representing air molecules) and passes a "sound wave" (shoulder tap) through the line. When the group representing a solid finishes passing the tap down first, all the kids suddenly understand.

Complex Thinking and Spontaneous Movement

New research indicates that the emergence of certain types of knowledge is deeply linked with the body's movements. For instance, finger counting, which integrates math concepts and sensorimotor action, is nearly universal. What begins as a visual and kinesthetic aid to children, often persists into adulthood because of the sensorimotor associations (Bahnmueller et al., 2014). New mathematical understanding can also emerge via movement. For example, without being conscious, children use rhythm to display mathematical similarities and distinctions as they touch, manipulate, explore, feel or hold three-dimensional geometrical solids. The rhythms that children display tend to reflect the exact geometrical properties of the objects themselves (Bautista et al., 2011; Sheets-Johnstone, 2009). Researchers now believe that rhythm constitutes an essential and irreducible dimension of mathematical communication, as well as an integral component of mathematical sense. These researchers found similar overlaps when they analyzed sounds that elementary school children made as they interacted with geometrical objects. The sounds kids made reflected the geometrical similarities and distinctions of the objects they manipulated (Bautista & Roth, 2012). One child, Nadia, had an "aha!" moment when she realized that the best way to categorize the shapes was based on the number of points they had. But a deeper analysis of Nadia's movements just before her "aha!" moment showed that her realization was enacted and expressed kinetically first. In other words, Nadia moved and talked herself into the knowing. This was observable well before she was consciously aware of the ideas that her body was enacting, and before she was able to articulate the ideas verbally (Bautista et al., 2011). Nadia's insight did not occur first "in her mind," but instead, her geometric knowing came via the evolutionary movement of her living body. In a sense, she merged with the objects to understand them. Similarly, my 4-year-old nephew, Henry, was recently experimenting with making paper boats and trying out which ones were most seaworthy in the pool. After his careful hypothesis testing, Henry wanted to explain to me the sinking versus floating of every design. He spontaneously transposed his own body into the action, saying "this part stayed dry" and pointing to his shoulder, "but this part started to sink" down by his legs. Embodying his own "boatness" allowed Henry to both understand and articulate his discoveries.

Cognitive scientists at the University of Chicago have discovered that movement can help students master complex math skills. In a groundbreaking series of studies, they asked a group of second graders to gesture when they explained their solutions to difficult math problems and asked a second group to just verbally explain the solutions. Children who were unable to solve the problems but were in the gesturing group tended to add new – and correct – problem-solving strategies to their repertoires. When children from the gesturing group attempted to solve difficult math problems later, they were significantly more likely to succeed than those in the non-gesturing group. This is probably because they had taken in and then explained their own process in a dynamic, active, multimodal manner. They were engaging more than one part of their brains at a time, making more complex neural networks (Broaders et al., 2007). Gesturing, like other movement, allows the learner's representation of a problem to be grounded in two arenas, perceptual and motor, thus making information more readily available when solving a problem later (Goldin-Meadow & Alibali, 2013). Classroom lessons featuring gestures are shown to promote deeper reasoning, synthesis and information retention than those that do not feature gestures (Goldin-Meadow & Alibali, 2013). One teacher gave children a lesson on liquid conservation, either with gestures or without gestures, referring to the height and width of the two glasses. Children who were instructed with gestures did better on later assessments than those who were instructed without the gestures (Ping & Goldin-Meadow, 2008).

Movement Outdoors

The outdoors is especially effective at offering children multimodal learning experiences because it is wildly dynamic. Experts say that young children should be outdoors as much as possible, and certainly as much they are indoors (White, 2008). Meanwhile, when given the choice, kids almost always prefer to be outside. The outdoors is a less predictable, more versatile and flexible place where children can explore, take some risks, respond to physical and social challenges and be in charge in a moving, changing milieu. Learning and playing outdoors offers children access to big spaces with opportunities to be their naturally exuberant physical and noisy selves. It affords them freedom from literal walls and boundaries to be adventuresome and be messy. It also offers them fresh air and direct experience with the elements, natural living things and movements of the surround – things that "make sense," using the senses. Outdoor activities also promote social cohesion, reduce the tendency toward conflicts and stimulate the development of a sense of autonomy and self-sufficiency (White, 2008).

We adults and teachers have sent a confusing and dualistic message to children: that the real work of the day, the work of the mind, happens indoors; while the outside is the place for the less serious work of the body, including play and physical education. Julie Mountcastle, Head of School at Slate School, believes that recess needs to be rebranded, since there is no hierarchy in value between indoor and outdoor, structured and unstructured learning. She advocates for asking young learners: "Where would this activity – for you – be the best?" It may make no sense to a teacher to need to do a math or an art project outside with one's toes in the grass, but for a child that sensory input may make all the difference in enjoyment and focus and learning.

Research is in our corner yet again – providing evidence for the many benefits of the outdoors for children's learning. In a recent study, a barren school ground was redesigned with gardens and an amphitheater for teaching and learning opportunities. One group of children had math and science classes outdoors, while a comparison group experienced the identical content in traditional indoor classrooms. The redesigned outdoor school kids had the highest levels of academic attainment. These kids reported more opportunities to explore, experiment and work collaboratively than the children in the traditional classroom (Khan et al., 2020). Another study followed a cohort of 562 Norwegian 3- to 7-year-olds, measuring cognitive and socioemotional effects and finding that attention deficit and hyperactivity symptoms significantly decreased as time spent outdoors in school increased (Ulset et al., 2017).

Walking

Walking is an ideal way to spend time outdoors. When we go for a walk, the heart pumps faster, circulating more blood and oxygen to the brain. Walking promotes new connections between brain cells, increases the volume of the hippocampus (a brain region involved with memory) and raises levels of molecules that both stimulate the growth of new neurons and transmit messages between them. The back-and-forth cadence and moving of the body rhythmically when walking is known make us feel emotionally better. This is because bilateral brain stimulation encourages communication and flow between different parts of the brain (Amano & Toichi, 2016). And walking has long been associated with better thinking and solving problems. Poet William Wordsworth is thought to have walked as many as 180,000 miles in his lifetime (Jabr, 2014). Einstein walked religiously – miles to and from the Princeton University campus every day. Queen Elizabeth, too, attributes her longevity and calm, clear-headedness to her brisk walks outdoors. Walking is also a cultural activity common in many indigenous communities across the globe (Marin, 2020). Teachers in outdoor schools have a simple rule of thumb: a child can walk 1 km (about ½ mile) for every year of life. It is not uncommon for preschool children around the world to walk 2–4 miles every day.

When we teach kids to walk and contemplate, we let the pace of their feet naturally synchronize with their breathing. They don't have to devote much conscious effort to this act; their attention is free to wander in an alert and receptive, mindful present. Such relaxed mental states are linked in experiments with innovative ideas and strokes of insight, as mentioned in the previous chapter. One exciting study invited students to complete the same creative, divergent thinking tasks while either sitting, walking on a treadmill, or sauntering through Stanford University's beautiful campus. When they were asked to generate atypical uses for everyday objects, like buttons or tires, the students averaged significantly more novel uses for the objects while walking than while seated (Oppezzo & Schwartz, 2014).

Nature

Fresh air, trees and a sunny day can do miracles for the human mind and spirit. It is no wonder that wise humans have recommended going into nature for insights through the ages: shamans finding answers in the wilderness, monks retreating to the desert to pray and Native Americans embarking on land-immersed vision quests. Nature heals and calms, reminding us of what really matters. Of course, the original kindergarten – "The Children's Garden" – conceived by Friedrich Fröebel in the 19th century was a designed as a school where children learned in nature (Sobel, 2020). We need to give kids more time and space to be on the land, in the sunshine and in the snow. Kurt Stanco, principal at CREC Discovery Academy, a public STEM magnet school, encourages his faculty to cancel their plans when it snows and to take the kids outside. "The best learning is outside when it snows, so since we have such snowy winters, we now focus on having enough winter gear on hand for every child" (K. Stanco, personal communication, July 25, 2021). Nature can help kids learn to be still and quiet, to notice the seasons changing and then respond to them in art or writing. Or, being immersed in the buzzing and humming of nature can encourage young children to run around and be wild and loud (Riley, 2020).

One homeschooling dad commented,

> Every time I go into nature with the children, even though it might start with some grumbling, as soon as we start looking around, something will grab their attention and then it's hard to leave. Last week, I took my son and daughter on a walk behind the house. I took them a little further than usual. My son was not happy, and trying to put as much ill will as possible into the walk. But just as we were turning around, one of us spotted a raspberry. Then we found heaps of them. And suddenly they were so focused on finding and picking raspberries. The funny thing is that my son doesn't even like raspberries! But I guess just the process of collecting as many as possible was exciting. We didn't have any containers so they made bowls using their shirts. Now, I was in a bit of a hurry. I had to get home to start working. But making them leave the raspberry field proved extremely difficult. I also wanted them to walk faster, but they wanted to go slow so as not to drop any berries. So, I was the grumpy one on the way back!

In Japan, the practice of *shinrin yoku*, or "forest bathing," has shown myriad benefits for humans of all ages. Exposure to better air quality, more colors, natural forms and natural ambient sounds strengthens the immune and respiratory systems, also decreasing heart rate, blood pressure and levels of the stress hormone cortisol. Forest bathers exhibit improved mood, lowered stress and less aggressiveness; and they display better intellectual performance, including better memory, following a forest bath (Mathias et al., 2020). Similarly, joggers who exercise outdoors in natural settings feel more restored and less anxious or angry than people who burn the same number of calories indoors. In a now classic experiment, environmental psychologists found that patients recovering from surgery next to bedside windows looking out over the leafy trees of a garden were healed a full day faster than their counterparts who looked out a brick wall. The patients with the garden view also needed significantly less pain medication and had fewer postsurgical complications (Ulrich, 1984).

Not all children have access to miles of woods or fields to roam in. But time outdoors is not necessarily about big spaces – anything with sunlight or snowflakes will do. Smaller urban outdoor landscapes can be just as dynamic and nourishing as more spacious rural ones. Some outdoor educators have coined the term "nearby nature" to capture the notion that that clump of trees at the end of the cul-de-sac, or the ravine behind the warehouse, is still teeming with nature potential. Though those places may seem insignificant at first glance, through a child's eyes a patch of grass can contain a whole universe, and in fact it does, if one takes the time to look more closely at everything happening under there (Volland, 2008).

Despite these benefits, research indicates that access to outdoor play for children continues to be diminished, largely due to access, safety, time and competing interests. Children are failing to develop a personal connection to the natural world, preferring instead to play inside with electronic devices (Dankiw et al., 2020). A startling example of a disconnect with nature was a recent survey of school children which found that 13 percent of 8- to 11-year-olds thought that pasta came from an animal, while one in ten 11- to 14-year-olds had no idea that carrots and potatoes grew underground (Skea & Fulford, 2021). Richard Louv coined the term Nature Deficit Disorder and has described the human costs of alienation from nature, including faded use of the senses, attention difficulties and higher rates of physical and emotional sickness. Data clearly shows that an absence of nature in children's lives contributes to rising rates of obesity, attention challenges and depression. On the other hand, kids who spend more time outdoors tend to do better on all cognitive and socioemotional measures – they do better in science, math and reading; they play more cooperatively with other children (Volland, 2008).

Be warned that our own agendas and lesson plans will almost always get cast aside when children are given freedom outside. Furthermore, kids' initial interactions with nature are not always reverent. Champions of environmental education sometimes cringe when they witness children crushing plants, picking flowers, squashing ant hills and hacking branches off trees. But it is only through encountering the natural world in an authentic way that kids get to know it intimately. Though scrappy at first, this will become the foundation of a respect and love for nature (Louv, 2012). If we never let children interact in their unformed, awkward ways, they will never arrive at any enlightenment. We must allow the growth to happen. It is a dialectic that is sometimes counterintuitive and often uncomfortable (C. LePage, personal communication, June 3, 2021).

How Dynamic Outdoor Learning Nourishes Social Justice

Naturalist Aldo Leopold (1949) famously argued, "We can be ethical only in relation to something we can see, feel, understand, love or otherwise have faith in" (p. 214). Thus, only when children are connected to the land can they look at what we're doing to the land and make more virtuous decisions about it. Intimate knowledge of local places and their existing problems leads to ownership and action to initiate change. Learning generated from these places can be translated into sustainable thinking and action. We must make learning relevant to the places in which we live – and do so in a manner that celebrates action (Straker et al., 2017). This is a call for an engaged learning in which place is not just a noun, but also a verb. Social and ecological justice issues will take center stage as students explore their roots and places outside the four walls of a classroom. Environmental education raises the level of critical thinking and reflection, allowing students to think about the future that they desire and how they wish to live in it. Learning outdoors and about their place in a situated ecosystem gets students in thinking about preserving ecosystems for future generations of humans (Webber, 2021).

The outdoors, whether in an unspoiled natural landscape, a managed town park or a patch of wildflowers in an industrial center, can open up the possibilities for understanding natural relationships, turning what was once a backdrop into an integral part of who we are. In the Mbya-Guarani communities of Argentina, for example, daily life includes deep interrelations among children, families, communities and the forest environment. They do not just live in the forest, they consider themselves – together with other living beings – part of this environment, which is essential for the continuity of the Mbya way of life. The unit of analysis for early childhood education there is the child-in-its-environment. As soon as the children become conscious of their environment, they are introduced to a culture of respect. Respect is given to all forms of life (Remorini, 2015).

Sample Nourishment of Embodied, Ecologically Attuned, Outdoor Learning

Learning outdoors adds complexity and dynamism to any lesson. Take, for example, a child painting a picture in a classroom. She gives her attention to the work, the colors and the design. But painting that same picture outdoors, the child is attentive in a different way: to the action of the wind on her paper, to how quickly the paint dries, to the uneven ground on which her paper rests, to the unfamiliar sounds of the outdoors as she paints. Becoming attentive in this way to what is unfamiliar opens up new ways of thinking about her world and her place in it (Skea & Fulford, 2021). In Germany, there are more than one thousand

Forest Kindergartens, many of which have no indoor facilities, but tents, shelters or yurts for a warm fire and protection from the elements. For the whole of their 6-hour day, 4- and 5-year-old Forest kindergarteners are outside. Research shows that they are healthier and have better physical and language development than their mostly indoor peers (Sobel, 2020). Forest schools have popped up all over the United States, at first as a way to learn in person during the Covid-19 pandemic, but lasting because of the enhanced engagement in children across all academic subjects. Similarly, in New Zealand, kids in Enviroschools programs spend most days outdoors, grounded in Māori culture and emphasizing a strong connectedness to place with a rich and meaningful relationship with the natural world (Alcock & Ritchie, 2018). These outdoor learning examples flip most educational models on their head. The norm is being educated indoors for upwards of 6–8-hours per day, with a half an hour outside at recess. What if instead we thought about the outdoors as a place to learn to read, do math, develop grit and perseverance? (Sobel, 2020).

Public school kindergarten teacher Eliza Minnucci in Quechee, Vermont, decided to implement a Forest Fridays program a few years ago. Her class completed their regular curriculum four days of the week, and then went outdoors in the forest (a 15-minute walk up into the woods) on Fridays. They did so year-round in all weather and were able to get donations of warm gear for winter months. One mother of a child in Ms. Minnucci's class noticed about her daughter:

> She has become increasingly more responsible at home and is taking it upon herself to do jobs that will help out. She is more confident in knowing she can take initiative to help instead of waiting to be asked to do something. I think that it would be great if all kids in the school could spend one day per week outside. This might provide an opportunity for kids in different grades to work together on projects out in the forest.
>
> Sobel, 2020, p. 1066

Another Vermont teacher, Jennifer Kramer, took inspiration from this program and implemented it with students with special needs. They went outside every Friday morning, taking a mile-long walk to a little-known piece of conservation land in their town. They would eat lunch in the woods and be back at school for the last two hours of the day. Ms. Kramer also noticed profound changes in her students. She had planned to simply conduct her lessons outside, asking students to measure the flow rate of the stream or to study forest management. But something more profound emerged. "They were learning, or in some cases relearning, to love being in the forest. And, to a person, they were happier. For some of them, this was the only day during the week they enjoyed school" (Sobel, 2020, pp. 1067–1068). They waded in streams, made crowns and bracelets, excavated a fire pit and cooked over the fire, made shrines for dead birds, built bridges, constructed forts. In the winter they tracked animals, had snowball fights. They made forts that became a village, and each fort developed its own clan, in response to ongoing fable-like stories that they told. The children-villagers then collected quartz stones from the stream to serve as their currency. Peeled bark from fallen trees became a prized natural resource since it was an effective rain-proofing material for fort roofs. Over time, the eagle, moose, coyote and bear clans each devised their own face paint pattern, applied with a black paint made from fire pit charcoal. They invented their own chants, made totem flags, shaped totem animal snow sculptures in the deep mid-winter to guard their forts. The creation of the clans led to the deepening of relationships that could not have happened in the classroom. Students had to problem solve, work out disputes, collaborate on technical innovations. And they had to contribute their labor to the service of the whole – collecting wood, agreeing about how to minimize environmental impact, developing contracts for how to keep everyone safe (Sobel, 2020).

Teachers sometimes worry that outside time will be less easy to manage; that the children will stray from control or safety, or that this type of learning diverts too far from state curriculum standards. Far from it. In fact, learning outdoors accomplishes learning outcomes in lots of home-grown ways. Like practical math problems: "If it's a mile from school down to the trailhead and it takes us 20 minutes to walk there, how many miles per hour are we walking?" or "For snack out in the woods today, if each person is going to want 6 ounces of lemonade and there are 25 people going, how many gallons of lemonade are we going to need? And how many quart containers are we going to need to transport that down there?" (Sobel, 2020).

A small patch of dirt, a single tree and a walk to the store are all opportunities to observe nature, generate questions and conduct science experiments to find answers. In fact, building understandings of everyday phenomena, such as why leaves fall from trees, where rain goes in a city and how city animals find shelter are key practices for the development of scientific thinking (Goldstein et al., 2018). Preschool teacher Leticia Howard might say to her class, "Look at these two puddles," pointing to one in the middle of the sunny sidewalk and another in the shade of their school building. "Which do you think will disappear first?" "Why?" The children can then predict whether more people will walk through that puddle and whether the sun will help it dry up faster. The children can use chalk to outline both puddles. The next day, they can check the puddles. Each time, children will draw increasingly smaller puddle outlines until the puddle in the middle of the sidewalk is gone entirely. Tallying and comparing the numbers of trees and cars in particular areas of the city, and then calculating whether there are enough trees to absorb the air pollution produced by the number of cars counted, is another urban idea for nature-based science learning (Goldstein et al., 2018). In all cases, learning outside can make use of low or no cost materials – for example, children can pour water from bottles to observe and compare how it flows on permeable surfaces like grass or soil, and impermeable surfaces like pavement. Follow up with questions like "What hard surfaces don't absorb water?" "Why can lots of rain be a problem for cities and towns?" or "What could carry the extra water out of the city?" are wonderful thought experiments that can be followed up with empirical study (Goldstein et al., 2018).

In Sum

As educators, we need to shift our framework of attention from an indoor, contained and passive model to an outdoor, active, embedded and embodied model. Findings from the laboratory – as well as evidence from our own classrooms – make it clear: movement is the best medium for harnessing and directing learning. Dynamic movement allows children to know their own bodies (a hallmark of self-regulation) and to trust their own gut feelings. This can create a confidence in vulnerable students to speak their truth to power. Further, children need to learn in spaces and places with the full sensory experiences available in nature. We cannot partition ourselves away from our bodies or away from our sense of literal groundedness. When we co-constitute our worlds, we will feel an intrinsic sense of responsibility. This necessitates more ethically situated commitment to how we might cultivate and sustain relationships with others (Riley, 2020).

References

Alcock, S., & Ritchie, J. (2018). Early childhood education in the outdoors in Aotearoa, New Zealand. *Journal of Outdoor and Environmental Education,21*(1), 77–88. https://doi.org/10.1007/s42322-017-0009-y

Amano, T., & Toichi, M. (2016). The role of alternating bilateral stimulation in establishing positive cognition in EMDR therapy: A multichannel near-infrared spectroscopy study. *PLOS One, 11*(10), e0162735. https://doi.org/10.1371/journal.pone.0162735

Bahnmueller, J., Dresler, T., Ehlis, A. C., Cress, U., & Nuerk, H. C. (2014). NIRS in motion—unraveling the neurocognitive underpinnings of embodied numerical cognition. *Frontiers in Psychology, 5*, 743. https://doi.org/10.3389/fpsyg.2014.00743

Bautista, A., & Roth, W. M. (2012). The incarnate rhythm of geometrical knowing. *The Journal of Mathematical Behavior, 31*(1), 91–104. https://doi.org/10.1016/j.jmathb.2011.09.003

Bautista, A., Roth, W. M., & Thom, J. S. (2011). Knowing, insight learning, and the integrity of kinetic movement. *Interchange, 42*(4), 363–388. https://doi.org/10.1007/s10780-012-9164-9

Broaders, S. C., Wagner Cook, S., Mitchell, Z. & Goldin-Meadow, S. (2007). Making children gesture brings out implicit knowledge and leads to learning. *Journal of Experimental Psychology: General, 136*(4), 539–550. https://doi.org/10.1037/0096-3445.136.4.539

Cajete, G., & Bear, L. L. (2000). *Native science: Natural laws of interdependence* (Vol. 315). Clear Light Publishers.

Cecchini, J. A., & Carriedo, A. (2020). Effects of an interdisciplinary approach integrating mathematics and physical education on mathematical learning and physical activity levels. *Journal of Teaching in Physical Education, 39*(1), 121–125. https://doi.org/10.1123/jtpe.2018-0274

Dankiw, K. A., Tsiros, M. D., Baldock, K. L., & Kumar, S. (2020). The impacts of unstructured nature play on health in early childhood development: A systematic review. *PLOS One, 15*(2), e0229006. https://doi.org/10.1371/journal.pone.0229006

Dotson-Renta, L. N. (2016). Why young kids learn through movement. *The Atlantic, 19* www.theatlantic.com/education/archive/2016/05/why-young-kids-learn-through-movement/483408/.

Galinsky, E. (2010). *Mind in the making: The seven essential life skills every child needs* (NAEYC special ed.). HarperCollins.

Glenberg, A. M. (2011). How reading comprehension is embodied and why that matters. *International Electronic Journal of Elementary Education, 4*(1), 5–18.

Goldin-Meadow, S., & Alibali, M. W. (2013). Gesture's role in speaking, learning, and creating language. *Annual Review of Psychology, 64*, 257–283. https://doi.org/10.1146/annurev-psych-113011-143802

Goldstein, M., Famularo, L., & Kynn, J. (2018). From puddles to pigeons: Learning about nature in cities. *Young Children, 73*(5), 42–50. www.jstor.org/stable/26783679

Gray, P. (2013). *Free to learn: Why unleashing the instinct to play will make our children happier, more self-reliant, and better students for life.* Basic Books.

Griss, S. (1994). Creative movement: A physical language for learning. *Educational Leadership, 51*(5), 78–80.

Imus, D. (2008). *Growing up green: Baby and child care.* Simon and Schuster.

Jabr, F. (2014). Why walking helps us think. *The New Yorker.* www.newyor ker.com/tech/annals-of-technology/walking-helps-us-think

Johnson-Glenberg, M. C., Megowan-Romanowicz, C., Birchfield, D. A., & Savio-Ramos, C. (2016). Effects of embodied learning and digital platform on the retention of physics content: Centripetal force. *Frontiers in Psychology, 7,* 1819. https://doi.org/10.3389/fpsyg.2016.01819

Khan, M., McGeown, S., & Bell, S. (2020). Can an outdoor learning environment improve children's academic attainment? A quasi-experimental mixed methods study in Bangladesh. *Environment and Behavior, 52*(10), 1079–1104. https://doi.org/10.1177/00139 16519860868

Leopold, A., & Schwartz, C. W. (1949). *A Sand County almanac, and sketches here and there.* Oxford University Press.

Louv, R. (2012). *The nature principle: Reconnecting with life in a virtual age.* Algonquin Books.

Marin, A. M. (2020). Ambulatory sequences: Ecologies of learning by attending and observing on the move. *Cognition and Instruction, 38*(3), 281–317. https://doi.org/10.1080/07370008.2020.1767104

Mathias, S., Daigle, P., Dancause, K. N., & Gadais, T. (2020). Forest bathing: A narrative review of the effects on health for outdoor and envir-onmental education use in Canada. *Journal of Outdoor and Environmental Education, 23*(3), 309–321. https://doi.org/10.1007/s42322-020-00058-3

Medina, J. (2012, November). *Educating diverse minds: Using indi-vidual brain differences to teach and reach all learners.* Keynote speech delivered at the 33rd Learning and the Brain Conference, Boston, MA.

Oppezzo, M., & Schwartz, D.L. (2014). Give your ideas some legs: The posi-tive effect of walking on creative thinking. *Journal of Experimental Psychology: Learning, Memory, and Cognition, 40*(4), 1142–1152. http://dx.doi.org/10.1037/a0036577

Ostroff, W. L. (2014). Don't just sit there: Pay attention! *Educational Leadership, 72*(2), 70–74.

Parnell, R., & Procter, L. (2011). Flexibility and placemaking for autonomy in learning. *Educational & Child Psychology, 28*(1), 77–88.

Pellegrini, A. D., Huberty, P. D., & Jones, I. (1995). The effects of play depriv-ation on children's recess and classroom behaviors. *American*

Educational Research Journal, *32*, 845–864. https://doi.org/10.3102/00028312032004845

Ping, R. M., & Goldin-Meadow, S. (2008). Hands in the air: using ungrounded iconic gestures to teach children conservation of quantity. *Developmental Psychology*, *44*(5), 1277. https://doi.org/10.1037/0012-1649.44.5.1277

Remorini, C. (2015). Learning to inhabit the forest: Autonomy and interdependence of lives from a Mbya-Guarani perspective. *Advances in Child Development and Behavior*, *49*, 273–288. https://doi.org/10.1016/bs.acdb.2015.09.003

Riley, K. (2020). Posthumanist and postcolonial possibilities for outdoor experiential education. *Journal of Experiential Education*, *43*(1), 88–101. https://doi.org/10.1177/1053825919881784

Rueda, M. R., Posner, M. I., & Rothbart, M.K. (2004). Attentional control and self-regulation. In R. F. Baumeister & K. D. Vohs (Eds.), *Handbook of self-regulation: Research, theory, and applications* (pp. 283–300). Guilford Press.

Schulte, P. (2005). Social studies in motion: Learning with the whole person. *Social Studies and the Young Learner*, *17*(4), 13–16.

Sheets-Johnstone, M. (2009). *The corporeal turn: An interdisciplinary reader*. Imprint Academic.

Skea, C., & Fulford, A. (2021). Releasing education into the wild: an education in, and of, the outdoors. *Ethics and Education*, *16*(1), 74–90. https://doi.org/10.1080/17449642.2020.1822612

Smith, C.P., King, B., & Hoyte, J. (2014). Learning angles through movement: Critical actions for developing understanding in an embodied activity. *The Journal of Mathematical Behavior*, *36*, 95–108. https://doi.org/10.1016/j.jmathb.2014.09.001

Sobel, D. (2020). School outdoors: The pursuit of happiness as an educational goal. *Journal of Philosophy of Education*, *54*(4), 1064–1070. https://doi.org/10.1111/1467-9752.12458

Straker, J., Potter, T. G., & Irwin, D. (2017). Untrodden paths: A critical conversation about wilder places in outdoor education. *Canadian Journal of Environmental Education*, *22*, 97–114.

Ulrich, R. (1984). View through a window may influence recovery from surgery. *Science*, *224*, 420–421. https://doi.org/10.1126/science.6143402

Ulset, V., Vitaro, F., Brendgen, M., Bekkhus, M., & Borge, A.I. (2017). Time spent outdoors during preschool: Links with children's cognitive and behavioral development. *Journal of Environmental Psychology*, *52*, 69–80. https://doi.org/10.1016/j.jenvp.2017.05.007

Viadero, D. (2008). Exercise seen as priming the pump for students' academic success. *Education Week*, *27*, 14–15. www.edweek.org/ew/articles/2008/02/13/23exercise_ep.h27.html?tmp=1797071541

Volland, A. (2008, February 13). Why kids need a big dose of nature. *U.S. News & World Report*. http://capitolcreek.com/foreverwildfilm/PDF/KidsNeed.pdf

Webber, G. (2021). The Terrain of place-based education. *Brock Education Journal*, *30*(1), 10–10.

White, H. (2008). Connecting today's kids with nature: A policy action plan (pp. I–27, Rep.). National Wildlife Federation. www.nwf.org/~/media/PDFs/Campus-Ecology/Reports/CKN_full_optimized.ashx

7

Empowering Young Children to Value All Voices, Practice Dialogue
How to Nourish Active, Deep Listening and Critical Thinking

It is tempting to assume that since children are newer to this world, and need care and direction, they have less complex and nuanced thoughts than adults. On the contrary, children experience life in such distinct and unusual ways that they have much to enrich the lives of others. Parents, teachers and even philosophers can benefit from emulating children's openness, challenge to convention and playful embrace of questioning. When we acknowledge children's contributions to thought – when we empower their perspectives via practices like dialogue – all of us together can gain deeper understanding and meaning. Further, practicing dialogue in the classroom allows children to develop the virtues we want them to have in order to become engaged, active citizens; to stand up for social justice. These skills include: valuing all voices, understanding and taking multiple perspectives,

DOI: 10.4324/9781003202875-8

holding disparate values and views, respecting diversity and listening actively.

Evolutionary and Developmental History of Dialogue

Dialogue is deep in us. The oral traditions of our ancestors took place not in passive silence, but in reflective listening: deliberating right and wrong, sharing experiences and wisdom and socially negotiating truth. Our large and intricate brains evolved to consider our common human condition, even as we were living it, which is neurologically complex skill indeed. There is nothing more delightful and illuminating than talking about big ideas with little people. Young children, like all humans, co-create knowledge. They thrive on connection, conversation, sharing insights and stories. Examining our worlds is the essence of humanity, and children can barely wait to share their thoughts, ideas and questions with others (Ostroff, 2020).

Conversation is a powerful and yet demanding skill. When we converse with others, one speaker talks at a time. Sure, we may interrupt or talk over one another very briefly, but most switches from one speaker to the next are nearly seamless – only 5 percent of human speech overlaps with another speaker. We may take this for granted, but in fact, a smooth transition in conversation requires tight and quick coordination between participants – most transitions are between 0 and 200 milliseconds, and most turns are only a few seconds long. This means that our verbal responses must be planned in the middle of the incoming turn (Levinson, 2016). Even though the languages of the world vary immensely (in terms of word ordering, the sounds and the grammatical organization), all languages seem to use rapid turn-taking (Stivers et al., 2009). Further, all branches of primates use turn-taking in their vocal communication, which suggests that turn-taking evolved before human language and may have provided a frame for its development. Babies participate in turn-taking long before they understand language or have spoken their first words. By 3 months old, infants interact with caretakers in cooperative and co-creative conversation-like exchanges. These "protoconversations" follow the same temporal patterns as adult conversation. Infants learn quickly how to mimic conversational timing, and when adults do not respond in a contingent fashion to their conversation-like eye contact, movement and sounds, infants become very upset (Hilbrink et al., 2015). Indeed, we are set up to communicate this way.

How Dialogue Facilitates and Deepens Learning

Picture a first-grade classroom with all of the children facing one another in a circle as their teacher, Mrs. Lopez, reads a story from the Arnold Lobel (1970) classic, *Frog and Toad Are Friends*. The children become immersed in the action and pictures as she reads, and then they start to respond to the text, to connect it to their own lives and experiences, including their own expertise in the topic at hand: friendship. (After all, who spends more time and energy negotiating with friends than kids do?) Suddenly the classroom is filled with energy, meaning and relevance, as student perspectives begin to take center stage over the teacher's (Lone & Burroughs, 2016). Children raise thoughts and questions in turn and begin to narrow to their own shared, key question, identified and highlighted by the teacher: "What makes someone a friend?" One child refers directly to the story: Toad was being a friend to Frog by sharing his cookies. Another child builds upon and questions the assumptions: "But wait, can't you share with someone who is not your friend?" Kids raise examples and counter-examples. They articulate their perspectives, describe and challenge points of view, all to make sense of their lived experience in response one another and to the text at hand (Chesters, 2012). Thus, the dialogue on friendship becomes philosophical. Children from a young age relish in philosophical questions and have seemingly endless energy for considering these questions with others. Classroom discussion is a powerful pedagogy for humans of all ages, but especially so for young children.

After some weeks of this practice, Mrs. Lopez begins to notice a shift: a deeper engagement with curricular topics in general. Mrs. Lopez's first graders also begin to focus on one another rather than on her. They mention that they were thinking about their conversations at home; that they asked their parents and siblings at dinner to consider what constitutes friendship or fairness or sharing. In class, they are genuinely interested in what their peers have to say; in fact, they can't wait to find out. Even still, they show patience while classmates struggle to articulate and express their complicated ideas. The students have become producers, not just consumers of knowledge, and they begin to connect the dots across individual discussions and pull out threads of deeper understanding, including understanding of their own thinking, the complex cognitive skill known as meta-cognition. The children in Mrs. Lopez's class know that in this space their concerns, worries, questions and ideas matter (Lone & Burroughs, 2016). These children have found their voice within dialogue. They have been empowered.

Children Ask the Most and the Best Questions

One of the earliest and most famous proponents of the power of learning through dialogue was the Greek philosopher Socrates. Nearly 2,500 years ago, Socrates was sentenced to death for corrupting the youth of Athens by inciting them to use *their own thoughts* to challenge the status quo. In one famous story, *The Meno*, Socrates asked his colleague's slave 50 questions about whether virtue can be taught or whether it is endowed by nature, leading the boy to arrive at insightful conclusions on his own. Indeed, Socrates' talent as a teacher lay not in imparting his accumulated knowledge (he was after all, famous for saying, "I only know that I know nothing"), but in asking probing and upending questions. And that is what Socrates and all young children have in common.

Young children are natural inquirers. And children's questions are remarkably unhindered by social convention. It does not matter whether the subject is delicate, trivial or deeply metaphysical. Kids want to know how, why, for what reason; they want origins of ideas and consequences of them. For example, a child told the Socrates story above might ask, "Why did Meno have a slave, anyhow? What was his slave's name? How could Socrates (the supposed best questioner of all), spend several hours with the boy, and not ask him his name? Come to think of it, how could Socrates not question the ethics of child slavery, or slavery in general?" These types of questions are the seeds of dialogue and the foundation for critical thinking. Since dialogue and discussion center on questions, and children are master questioners (to use a Socratic syllogism), then children are uniquely suited for dialogue and discussion (Ostroff, 2020).

As discussed in Chapter 3, the development of questioning skills is important for the development of thinking. Parents and teachers can engage with children's own questions to frame a learning situation and to encourage them to reflect more deeply, thus stretching that child's learning. Studies show that as an individual child develops, his or her questions become both significantly more prolific and significantly more complex when scaffolded in this way (Frazier et al., 2009). In a dialogue, questions from peers or the facilitator almost always spur some kind of analysis from the child. This can lead to greater clarity about a concept, plus awareness of connections to other concepts and acknowledgement of different perspectives or assumptions. Questioning our own questions allows us to tentatively accept some answers, rule out others lacking in support and change our minds when presented with compelling evidence. That is why dialogue is an ideal exercise for developing children's thinking.

Like Socrates, children assume that they don't know much. By seamlessly avoiding that counterproductive adult urge to appear knowledgeable, kids' minds are wide open for learning (Bjorklund, 2007). This allows the child take more stabs at understanding, more "shots on the basket," to create more opportunity for practice. Teacher Marietta McCarty (2006) has run philosophy seminars in elementary school classrooms for more than 20 years, facilitating discussions on topics ranging from responsibility, to free will, to death. She says that kids thrive in complex dialogue precisely because of their rare combination of being articulate and uninhibited, a special blend of experience and innocence that makes nothing off limits to ask. In other words: kids are natural philosophers.

In the Present, Real-Time

Another reason that children are ideal discussion members is that they reside in the present moment. As self-important adults, our minds are often cluttered with our own struggles and narratives. But engaged kids aren't usually checking the clock and thinking of their lengthy list of things to do. They can very readily drop into play-mode, get carried away or fall into a flow state (with its concomitant deep engagement and learning) (Csikszentmihalyi, 1990). Being in the moment opens up the way that the human mind responds to things.

Dialogue is like improv – participants have to be ready to respond in real time to unanticipated twists and turns of topics, others' ideas and their own new insights, all happening live. Being present is the key to success. Like other creative endeavors, discussion cannot be scripted or planned, and almost anything can happen. Graphic novelist (and MacArthur Genius Award recipient) Lynda Barry believes that instructors who try to plan creative experiences are vastly misunderstanding the process.

> They start by telling them how important the paper is. You don't want to waste paper. So, you want to sit and think carefully about what it is you're going to draw before you draw it … That's not how drawing works at all.
>
> Lehoczky, 2019

The same can be said for planning in advance what you are going to say in a dialogue. Like a jazz club improv session, we have no idea where any given dialogue is going to go because it's dynamic and emergent. It is an embodied practice that works best when the participants are playful and in the moment. Improv-like skills, such as dialogue, are powerful for learning because they activate a very complex network of both prefrontal brain regions and premotor and lateral regions, brain networks needed for cognitive control *and* spontaneous thought, a cognitively challenging balance indeed (Beaty, 2015). Not only that, but teachers' and students' prefrontal brain activity simultaneously synchronizes during Socratic dialogues (Holper et al.,

2013). On the level of individual brains, and on the level of group dynamics, the magic of dialogue is more than the sum of its parts.

Active and Deep Listening

Dialogue is first about learning to listen in general – to put your own thinking on pause for a minute and truly hear what someone else has said. But ultimately, dialogue becomes about how to engage with people who hold different perspectives and opinions from your own, or different from those to which you have been exposed. As teachers, we can actively listen to young people and support their capacity to be civic agents in the world, who challenge problems with patience and creativity (Serriere et al., 2017).

When Jessie Stern was a young child, she told her mother everything – what she thought about particular colors, dreams she had about a big volcano, even her most outlandish ideas (like the plan to circumnavigate the globe in a hot air balloon). When something seemed important to her daughter – even if ridiculous from an adult's perspective – Jessie's mom would pause and truly listen to what Jessie had to say. Her presence was full and felt, without interruption, correction, opinions or advice. She allowed long silences while Jessie gathered her thoughts. Sometimes she asked questions, but mostly, she listened. Jessie believes that her mother's gift of quiet attention allowed her to develop a lasting capacity to trust others and to feel confident in her own voice. It also nourished a thirst to hear others' views and a curiosity about their stories, which has led to a career in journalism. But most of all, it taught her the art of deep listening (Stern & Samson, 2021).

Practicing dialogue strengthens the skills of active and deep listening. In a culture of soundbites and rush, these are virtues which have been somewhat lost. To grow skilled, deep listeners, we must first teach children to resist the urge to translate each thing they hear into something familiar. But instead, to just sit with difference. Active listening is not an easy cognitive task; our brains are efficiency organs, after all. This is why it is all the more important to develop listening skills early as a habit of mind. Listening without deciding how you will respond, or comparing what was said to your own views and perspectives, requires an active hold on the automatic desire to quickly evaluate and "make sense" of everything.

According to Zen master Thich Nhat Hanh, when we truly listen to others, we do it to help them to empty their hearts. Thus, even if they say things that are incorrect or silly, we continue to listen with openness and compassion. We can learn so much about our children and students through this practice. Dialogue is the practice children need to hone this powerful skill of attention plus compassion (Stern & Samson, 2021). In discussion, we need to encourage children to slow down and really hear what each speaker says. (Facilitators can help this process by asking a child to repeat someone else's ideas: "What did Sonia just say?"; or to metacognitively articulate: "Sonia thinks baseball is the most fun, but I think basketball is.") Other activities like whisper games, taking a "listening walk," identifying hidden noises, and describing the story behind a song they have just heard can help budding deep listeners (McShane & Jones, 1990).

How Dialogue Nourishes Social Justice

Kids' lives are almost fully managed by adults in educational, familial and social settings. They typically have zero say in policies, even when those policies directly impact their every hour and their own well-being. But children can participate as competent social actors in society, who champion their own perspectives. When we regard children as thinking persons, as opposed to passive learners, we give them the opportunity to regard themselves differently, as emerging citizens and worthwhile contributors in their own right and in their own words (Lone & Burroughs, 2016). And of course, when adults take children more seriously in school, children begin to take themselves more seriously as learners.

In a democratic society, it is not sufficient for individuals to be good thinkers who stand up for their values. They also need to be able to understand and evaluate one another's thinking; to be able to empathize with views that are divergent from their own, and to compromise (Serriere et al., 2017). Active citizens can articulate thoughtful opinions, but also question and challenge their own opinions; they can enter dialogue with others and get involved in public debate and actions. The United Nations has called upon children and young people to increase their authentic engagement in social institutions and to behave as critical agents of change. Further, children have spoken out about the need to be noticed and the desire to demonstrate their knowledge; to be regarded as capable peers, thinkers and researchers (Maynard et al., 2021).

Children Need to Be Empowered in Education

Dialogue is one of few pedagogies that truly empowers and transforms learners. We need to give children the opportunity to be in charge of their learning in this way, and let them know that their voices matter. Kids are the most important to empower, as they are swiftly disenfranchised by hierarchical models of education. One of my former students, a kindergarten teacher, noticed that in just one year of school (the step up from transitional kindergarten at 4 years old, to kindergarten at 5 years old), her students had already been socialized to inhibit their sharing and questioning.

Furthermore, recent research showed that it did not take long for young children to feel and enact implicit racism, sexism and violence, when it was present in their worlds. We must open space for teachers to notice and deconstruct classroom practices that privilege white, male dominance as normal and natural (Pacini-Ketchabaw & Berikoff, 2008). We need to hear from kids, and listen to their genuine interactions, in order to be vigilant with interrupting hegemonic and harmful narratives. We must also allow them to challenge our biases as adults and teachers, which we may be unaware of. Indeed, when students ask questions, make decisions together and solve problems, they begin to form their own values (Tredway, 1995). Only when children get the message that their voices count can they gain a sense of belonging and active participation in their community.

Revolutionary educational philosopher Paolo Freire (1993) believed that active dialogue (of the type that flattens hierarchies between teachers and students) was the only way to undo the oppression of racism, classism and sexism and create good citizens in a democracy. He distinguished dialogic or "problem-posing" education from "banking education," with the former requiring active participation and meaning making by all members of the group, and the latter hinging on teacher-centered approaches that deliver content in a "static, compartmentalized and predictable ways" (Freire, 1993, p. 71). Freire firmly believed that the teachers should learn from the students just as much as the students should learn from the teachers. Knowledge is created together in this way, with every form of wisdom that is brought to the table being equally validated.

To conduct dialogue with children in a Freirean way, parents and teachers must give up authority and challenge the assumptions typically made about children. Children can be empowered to share their own expertise by forming and standing up for their original thoughts. It takes courage to speak up, and this courage nourishes the regard of their unique contributions as valuable and deserving of respectful treatment (Lone & Burroughs, 2016). Dialogue, by its very nature, unsettles traditional teacher–student roles and creates a different dynamic between adults and children, one of recognition and respect as fellow thinkers, contemplating questions that are equally perplexing and important to all involved (Lone & Burroughs, 2016).

How Dialogue Nourishes Multiple Perspective-Taking

Educational institutions can tend to mirror the power dynamics at play in the larger society (Lone & Burroughs, 2016). Thus, in the classroom, a person's social identity (e.g., as a female, as Latino, as extroverted, as neurotypical) impacts one's status as a "knower." Knowers' perspectives and points of view, their expertise, are typically given more respect and air-time in school discussions. Traditional top-down classroom communication can silence particular children and fail to regard them as knowers (a role that is most often reserved for the teacher and privileged children). As children grow up, they increasingly receive messages about themselves that may be biased, to the point where they may stop believing they have anything interesting to add. Thus, a child's own perceived social group stereotypes can deprive him or her of the opportunity for authentic participation in the classroom, leading to lowered motivation, less comprehension and shallower learning. Such outcomes have been consistently documented in the school performance of kids belonging to disadvantaged groups (Lone & Burroughs, 2016). This plays out in dramatic and lasting ways – it is estimated that 85 percent of children in juvenile detention facilitates cannot read, write or otherwise communicate well – certainly not the classroom "knowers" – these are children who have gone unnoticed at best, and at worst have been regarded as the teachers' adversaries (Thorsen, 2019). We must actively disrupt such biases.

Dialogue is a natural vehicle to flipping such unconscious power dynamics. By prioritizing multiple perspectives and equal participation right from the get-go, dialogue lessens classroom invisibility, marginalization and structured silence. Listening to others, sharing thoughts and articulating one's own ideas are all benefits of dialogue. Moreover, the ability to consider others' perspectives and values at a young age jumpstarts empathy development in early childhood. Research shows that taking others' points of view can help children in myriad ways, including persevering on tasks, self-regulation and other executive functioning skills (White et al., 2017). In one recent study, scientists examined the effects of multiple perspective-taking on children's executive functioning performance. Five-year-olds' performance improved as their ability to distance from their own point of view increased. They performed best when making decisions as if they were another person. They also demonstrated greater self-control when taking a some-what distanced outsider's perspective on the self through third-person speech (White & Carlson, 2015). Taking multiple perspectives also promotes objective, big picture evaluations (Trope & Liberman, 2010).

When dialogue highlights our differences in opinions, values and experiences, it may at first feel uncomfortable. But we can show children that this discomfort is actually enlarging their understanding – discomfort is, after all, a prerequisite for genuine growth! However, the discomfort of difference swiftly shifts to the opportunity for children to learn empathy, social cohesion, tolerance and acceptance (Braster & Dronkers, 2013).

We need to remind kids how important it is to cultivate a discussion space with many perspectives. The more diverse the voices, the richer the dialogue will be. Intellectual modesty among children also helps. That is, the sense that all members of the group are fallible and all could be mistaken. When we introduce kids to the notion that everyone's perspectives are somehow influenced by privilege and/or disadvantage, we open them up to respectful questioning of all views, even their own. This can break down barriers inculcated in children from the broader society – including the implicit messages often given to lower-SES kids that they should defer to authority in school (Lone & Burroughs, 2016).

Talking and Thinking Together

Kids are constantly engaged in talk and other forms of social interaction. They even use private speech to talk themselves through complex cognitive situations. When children share information and coordinate socially, including working together to solve problems, they "interthink," combining their intellects in creative ways that add up to more than the sum of the parts. Thinking together is an important part of learning, but it has traditionally been ignored or even punished in school. Talk between learners in the classroom is most often treated as disruptive. Even in child-centered approaches that stress the autonomy of children, the significance of collaborative talk has tended to be downplayed in favor of individual performance (Mercer & Littleton, 2007).

For one thing, talking can help children handle complex emotional experiences and topics. Children become competent dealing with powerful emotions through interaction. Our youngest learners perceive teachers', caregivers' and peers' verbal and emotional responses during heightened situations, and then can interpret them using language. In one research study, preschoolers' knowledge of emotions corresponded to how thoughtfully their mothers talked about their feelings and emotions with them (Dunsmore & Karn, 2001). Children can also gain a richer understanding of their feelings, and how to regulate them, when they discuss literature that involves characters responding to emotional situations. Kids would be so well served if we could talk about uncomfortable, difficult and even negative emotions in school (Beardslee et al., 2014). Raising painful issues in a safe and captivating way, young children can practice expressing their feelings honestly and appropriately. It can be hard for caregivers and teachers to navigate difficult and complex issues with young children. But our own discomfort with sadness, anger, worry, violence and trauma only makes these feelings much harder for children to negotiate themselves (Beardslee et al., 2014).

In traditional school dialogues or discussions, children are asked their opinions or thoughts in a one-off exchange of information occurring between just that child and their teacher (Lone & Burroughs, 2016). Classroom dialogue is completely different from these kinds of didactic exchanges and is instead concerned with real-time problem solving, genuine meaning making and new ways of thinking and understanding. In dialogue, exchanges of information are mere launching points for exploring concepts, ideas and questions in a rigorous way, and ultimately seeking multiple truths rather than one correct answer (Dunlop & de Schrijver, 2018). Further, dialogue exercises all of the complex cognitive skills (and corresponding brain functions) that we know to enhance school performance in children, including executive functions such as planning, problem solving, negotiating rules and being flexible, and self-regulation skills such as inhibition, emotion regulation and sustaining attention (Vitiello & Greenfield, 2017). In one important research study, elementary aged children who practiced dialogue in school over an extended period not only scored better on standardized tests in English and mathematics but also significantly out-performed same-grade peers in tests of confidence, resilience, co-operation and empathy, engagement with different opinions and attitudes toward learning (Siddiqui et al., 2017).

How to Implement Dialogue with Young Children

A group of teacher-scholars from the Pennsylvania State University engaged in a series of dialogues with kindergarten students using the picture book *Hey, Little Ant* by Phillip and Hannah Hoose. This children's book presents an ethical dilemma in which an ant steals food from a boy and the boy has to decide whether or not to squash the ant. After reading the book, Mr. Burroughs set up the discussion by asking the children to close their eyes and imagine what it might be like to be an ant. He had them embody the perspective of one ant in particular, the one in the book who stole food from humans. Would the humans let him have some food? Would they crush him? Students started to share their interpretations of the text. "It's not ok to kill the ant, because we are all animals – he is not so different from us," said Rose. Several students agreed with her, and some took the opposite view. Jack said, "You can't take food. That's stealing." One student, Eric, offered up quite a different perspective: "I think it's in the middle because they have no food left. The ant is in the middle. There's stealing, but probably they don't have a lot of food." In contemplating the ant's actions from multiple viewpoints, the children rejected the simple right versus wrong binary and came to a more rich and nuanced understanding of the complexity of the ethical issue. The kids agreed and disagreed with one another and considered the feelings of the ant and those of the boy, with several students settling on being "in the middle" regarding the ant's act of stealing. They began to discover how ethical dilemmas can be very complicated; that more than one choice may be defensible. The triumph of this dialogue was not that it got the children to think in a particular way about the ant's life, but rather that it got them to explore their own perspectives alongside those of others, giving varying views equal value, a skill that will serve them well in their role as critical and democratic citizens (Serriere, Burroughs & Mitra, 2017). As pioneering developmental psychologist Jean Piaget noted, "true discussion is only possible amongst equals" (Piaget, 1932, p. 409).

In Sum

Classroom dialogue is a truly revolutionary pedagogical tool. A great discussion is one of the best ways to engage people of all ages, to make visible student learning and to create community. Even the youngest students can do this, but if they are not used to taking charge of their own learning, it will take time and practice. They will need to break ingrained hierarchies, like looking to the teacher for the right questions and answers, or raising hands to speak. When learners respond to questions from a place of genuine interest (rather than trying to please teachers), they use entirely different networks of their brains (Kang et al., 2009). Students in a dialogue-based classroom will need to build those neural connections and open up their minds to new ways of being together. For that reason, dialogue is not a "one-off" experience to try – but rather a habit of mind and heart, a way of classroom life to nourish over weeks, months or years.

For teachers, the practice of dialogue will also take some time to get used to. In dialogue, we are no longer in charge of the classroom in the traditional way. For one thing, the students in a dialogue speak to one another freely, without raising hands, and look at one another, rather than at the teacher. Every voice in a discussion is equally valued and important, and everyone's experience is equally valid, regardless of background or school performance outside of the discussion. We learn to listen carefully to one another, and listen with deference. Part of the magic of dialogue is the playful "not-knowing" that opens us up to new experiences. Indeed, in a seminar discussion, it is okay to respectfully question everything – beginning with our own definitions, perspectives and biases, then those of our authors and those of each other. The teacher's role is both to create the environment in which this can happen and to ensure that the children's ideas build upon one another. We need to loosen our plans and get comfortable with not knowing exactly what will happen in class when practicing dialogue. There is no way to avoid a bit of chaos at first with this redistribution of power. But when a dialogue group truly connects, and launches into authentic deep learning, there is nothing more thrilling! Faith in the learning process is the key, and this comes from the confidence that dialogue has been an ideal way to transform students across cultures and throughout thousands of years.

References

Beardslee, W. R., Bartlett, J. D. & Ayoub, C. (2014). Tell me a story: A literacy-based intervention to help children, early care providers and parents talk about difficult topics. *Zero to Three*, *34*(6), 37–45.

Beaty, R. E. (2015). The neuroscience of musical improvisation. *Neuroscience and Biobehavioral Reviews*, *51*, 108–117. https://doi.org/10.1016/j.neubiorev.2015.01.004

Bjorklund, D.F. (2007). *Why youth is not wasted on the young: Immaturity in cognitive development*. Wiley-Blackwell.

Braster, S., & Dronkers, J. (2013). The positive effects of ethnic diversity in class on the educational performance of pupils in a multiethnic European metropole. *Education and Society*, *33*(2), 25–49. https://doi.org/10.7459/es/33.2.03

Chesters, S. D. (2012). *The Socratic classroom: Reflective thinking through collaborative inquiry*. Sense Publishers.

Csikszentmihalyi, M. (1990). *Flow: The psychology of optimal experience*. Harper Perennial.

Dunlop, L., & de Schrijver, J. (2018). Can a rabbit be a scientist? Stimulating philosophical dialogue in science classes. *School Science Review*, *99*(368), 35–43.

Dunsmore, J. C., & Karn, M. A. (2001). Mothers' beliefs about feelings and children's emotional understanding. *Early Education and Development*, *12*(1), 117–138. https://doi.org/10.1207/s15566935eed1201_7

Freire, P. (1993). *Pedagogy of the oppressed*. Continuum.

Frazier, B. N., Gelman, S. A., & Wellman, H. M. (2009). Preschoolers' search for explanatory information within adult–child conversation. *Child Development*, *80*, 1592–1611. https://doi.org/10.1111/j.1467-8624.2009.01356.x

Hilbrink, E. E., Gattis, M., & Levinson, S. C. (2015). Early developmental changes in the timing of turn-taking: A longitudinal study of mother–infant interaction. *Frontiers in Psychology*, *6*, 1492. https://doi.org/10.3389/978-2-88919-825-2

Holper, L., Goldin, A. P., Shalóm, D. E., Battro, A. M., Wolf, M., & Sigman, M. (2013). The teaching and the learning brain: A cortical hemo-dynamic marker of teacher–student interactions in the Socratic dialog. *International Journal of Educational Research*, *59*, 1–10. https://doi.org/10.1016/j.ijer.2013.02.002

Hoose, P. & Hoose, H. (1998). *Hey, little ant*. Tricycle Press.

Kang, M. J., Hsu, M., Krajbich, I., Loewenstein, G., McClure, S. M., Wang, J. T., & Camerer, C. F. (2009). The wick in the candle of learning: Epistemic curiosity activates reward circuitry and enhances memory. *Psychological Science*, *20*(8), 963–973. https://doi.org/10.1111/j.1467-9280.2009.02402.x

Lehoczky, E. (2019). Cartoonist Lynda Barry: Drawing "has to come out of your body." NPR. www.npr.org/2019/11/27/782921983/cartoonist-lynda-barry-drawing-has-to-come-out-of-your-body

Levinson, S. C. (2016). Turn-taking in human communication–origins and implications for language processing. *Trends in Cognitive Sciences*, *20*(1), 6–14. https://doi.org/10.1016/j.tics.2015.10.010

Lobel, A. (1970). *Frog and toad are friends*. Harper & Row.

Lone, J. M., & Burroughs, M. D. (2016). *Philosophy in education: Questioning and dialogue in schools*. Rowman & Littlefield.

McCarty, M. (2006). *Little big minds: Sharing philosophy with kids*. Penguin.

McShane, E. A., & Jones, E. L. (1990). Modifying the environment for children with poor listening skills. *Academic Therapy*, *25*(4), 439–446.

Mercer, N., & Littleton, K. (2007). *Dialogue and the development of children's thinking: A sociocultural approach*. Routledge.

Maynard, E., Barton, S., Rivett, K., Maynard, O., & Davies, W. (2021). Because "grown-ups don't always get it right": Allyship with children in research – from research question to authorship. *Qualitative Research in Psychology*, *18*(4), 518–536. https://doi.org/10.1080/14780887.2020.1794086

Ostroff, W. L. (2020). Empowering children through dialogue and discussion. *Educational Leadership*, *77*(7), 14–20.

Pacini-Ketchabaw, V., & Berikoff, A. (2008). The politics of difference and diversity: From young children's violence to creative power expressions. *Contemporary Issues in Early Childhood*, *9*(3), 256–264. https://doi.org/10.2304/ciec.2008.9.3.256

Piaget, J. (1932). *The moral judgement of the child*. Routledge.

Serriere, S. C., Burroughs, M. D., & Mitra, D. L. (2017). Kindergartners and "philosophical dialogue": Supporting child agency in the classroom. *Social Studies and the Young Learner*, *29*(4), 8–12.

Siddiqui, N., Gorard, S., & See, B. H. (2017). Non-cognitive impacts of philosophy for children. Project Report. School of Education, Durham University. https://dro.dur.ac.uk/20880/1/20880.pdf

Stern, J., & Samson, R. (2021, January 13). The gift of deep listening: How your presence and attention can impact those you love. *Psychology Today*. www.psychologytoday.com/us/blog/the-heart-and-scie nce-attachment/202101/the-gift-deep-listening

Stivers, T., Enfield, N. J., Brown, P., Englert, C., Hayashi, M., Heinemann, T., Hoymann, G., Rossano, F., de Ruiter, J. P., Yoon, K-E., & Levinson, S. C. (2009). Universals and cultural variation in turn-taking in conversation. *Proceedings of the National Academy of Sciences*, *106*, 10587–10592. https://doi.org/10.1073/pnas.0903616106

Thorsen, A. (2019, October 29). Dyslexia's part in the school-to-prison pipeline: The inequality inherent in our education system. *Dyslexia Untied*. https://dyslexia-untied.com/2019/10/29/dyslexias-part-in-the-school-to-prison-pipeline-the-inequality-inherent-in-our-education-system/

Tredway, L. (1995). Socratic seminars: Engaging students in intellectual discourse. *Educational Leadership*, *53*(1), 26–29.

Trope, Y., & Liberman, N. (2010). Construal-level theory of psychological distance. *Psychological Review*, *117*(2), 440. https://doi.org/10.1037/a0018963

Vitiello, V. E., & Greenfield, D. B. (2017). Executive functions and approaches to learning in predicting school readiness. *Journal of Applied Developmental Psychology*, *53*, 1–9. https://doi.org/10.1016/j.app dev.2017.08.004

White, R. E., & Carlson, S. M. (2015). What would Batman do? Self-distancing improves executive function in young children. *Developmental Science*, *19*(3), 419–426. http://doi.org/10.1111/desc.12314

White, R. E., Prager, E. O., Schaefer, C., Kross, E., Duckworth, A. L., & Carlson, S. M. (2017). The "Batman effect": Improving perseverance in young children. *Child Development*, *88*(5), 1563–1571. https://doi.org/10.1111/cdev.12695

Woodson, J., & Muth, J. (2002). *Our Gracie aunt*. Jump at the Sun Press.

Conclusion

This is an important moment in our history: a time ripe for meaningful change. We have been through years of a global pandemic at the same time as the #MeToo and Black Lives Matter social movements. Teachers are increasingly burdened, burned out and despondent. In a 2022 survey of teachers by the National Education Association (the largest teacher's union in the U.S.), over half said that they planned to leave the profession (Kamenetz, 2022). We can no longer tread the well-worn paths – we must now question all of the social facts surrounding our education systems. Sometimes the greatest tragedies and challenges can crack open equally great possibilities.

When I watched as a vandalizing and murderous mob stormed the United States Capitol Building in January 2021, something sank in me. It seemed that no matter what one's political views were, we had failed as a democracy if citizens who disagreed felt moved to violence. As a teacher and developmental psychologist, my sickness and despair moved to rethinking the ways we teach and learn. How can we grow young children, I tried to imagine, who can handle vastly different views peacefully and constructively? What if citizens felt empowered throughout their lives, and right from the get-go? I wondered how we might reimagine education from a backward integrated design perspective, asking: what skills do we want our learners to have when they have been "educated"? Can we generate thoughtful, engaged citizens who have empathy

DOI: 10.4324/9781003202875-9

for others – kids who can handle discomfort and conflict in fruitful and mutually beneficial ways, who are seasoned at questioning hierarchy and misuses of power and who aren't afraid to confront it with their minds and hearts? How do we get there? I realized that we need to start by examining how such virtues and skills emerge over evolutionary and developmental time. And then, we need to leverage those virtues and skills, and optimize for them. Only then can we equip children for the very real challenges they will face in the world they will inherit.

Navigating Complexity

In our rapidly changing world, some groups are unfairly privileged over others because of race, ethnicity, gender, class, language, religion, ability or age. We must unsettle those groups who have unjustly held power for so long. Today, approximately 40 percent of students in U.S. schools are from African, Asian, Latino and Native American ethnic groups. In urban schools, 63 percent of the student population consists of students of so-called minorities; in areas on the outskirts of cities, 36 percent; and in small towns and rural areas, 20 percent (National Center for Education Statistics, n.d.). Extending the demographic lens beyond the United States, Asians and Africans compose nearly 75 percent of the world's population, 60 percent and 14 percent, respectively (World Almanac Education Group, 2006). It makes sense to rethink the white, western lens through which our education systems were designed. Further, educational institutions are deeply politicized. In the late 1950s, entire school districts were shut down in response to the 1954 desegregation order, as some white folks in power elected to have no public schooling at all rather than integrate (McGee, 2021). The standards-based accountability movement in the 1990s and 2000s (including *No Child Left Behind* and *Race to the Top* legislation) was also highly political, because states and the federal government focused on outputs of standardized test scores by subgroups rather than on growing funding gaps in public education (Darling-Hammond & Oakes, 2019). Right now, we are seeing the demonization of critical race theory, the blocking of classroom discussion on gender identity and sexual orientation, and a staggering increase in banned books, resulting in state laws prohibiting teachers in many states from giving their students an honest view on history (Harris & Alter, 2022; Sawchuk, 2021; Wong, 2021).

We cannot in good faith shield children from this complexity – they are very aware of and sensitive to complicated relationships, to unfairness, to power differentials and distressing situations. And we don't want to insulate young children from the realities of the world. If we don't talk to them about the nuances that they perceive, they worry alone. When we pin fantasies of innocence on children, this distances us from kids' authentic lived experience and shields them from tough processes (like conflict resolution, or standing up for an underdog) and tough content (like environmental devastation, or our racist histories). Likewise, when we don't offer children the tools to handle aggression, discomfort and injustice, they are at sea when these things inevitably arise in their midst. Ultimately, our fantasies of innocent childhood cause real kids harm (Sonu, 2020).

Children are excited to delve into complexity and they are ready for social justice teaching and learning. When they are practiced at growing together, they become primed for understanding, valuing and empathizing with their fellow humans in a fair and just manner. They feel an intrinsic sense of responsibility and commitment to their relationships with others. When children get to play freely, they become savvy at the power negotiations that play demands. Dynamic movement allows children to know their own bodies (a hallmark of self-regulation) and to trust their own gut feelings. When children are encouraged to ask questions and their questions are honored, they burst forth with divergent thinking and creativity and they earnestly confront the injustices in our political and social realities. Likewise, when children are put in charge of their own unstructured and non-linear timeframes, they gain in patience, presence and comfort with discomfort. When kids have a say in how they learn and what they learn – when they have a voice – they thrive in multiple perspective-taking and critical thinking. They gain the confidence to speak their truth to power. They do so with joy and passion.

On the Ground

As the stewards of child growth and development, we will be asked to have immense patience and faith in empowering young children. We will have to challenge our own desires and attachments and become guides on the side, scaffolding rather than imparting knowledge. Our beautifully crafted plans will get cast aside as kids begin using the materials in their own creative ways. They will use and reuse many pieces of drawing paper during art, they will find unpredicted results in the science experiments and their characters in stories will behave in uncharacteristic ways. They will stick their fingers in the butter during cooking. The process of empowered and authentic learning is rarely linear or neat. When my son struggled unsuccessfully to join a pickup soccer game at the park, it was painful for me to see; and when my daughter and her friend tried to clean the kitchen after a day of baking cakes, the mess was so big that they couldn't nearly get it clean, despite their most focused efforts. However, these half attempts, these partial successes, are how kids build skills and eventually, wisdom.

Despite how it might first feel to enter this uncharted territory, we must put children's own ideas and interests and negotiations at the heart of the curriculum. Every teacher has struggled to get kids to learn something – things that they feel the kids must learn, or content and skills that they are required to teach them. When children are being forced to learn, both the teachers and the kids become stressed, because it is virtually impossible to make someone engage in something they are uninterested in. But if the learning situation is on the kids' own terms – if they want to learn something – it makes the job so much easier (Engel, 2021). If we want children to understand fair and unfair treatment, for instance, their own experience of being left out of a birthday party is of the highest relevance. Everyone benefits when we "ride the waves" of children's authentic concerns and experiences. Whatever they are interested in *is* the most important for them to learn.

Final Thoughts: Nourishing Virtuous Citizens, Leaders and Changemakers

Great leaders and changemakers have many virtues in common. They are critical thinkers and deep listeners, they are attuned with their environments, they are patient and present and they care deeply about others. Our role models have the courage to experiment and innovate. They are flexible and unrattled by unpredicted events. They lead with confidence and self-determination. The cognitive science and developmental psychology research shows unequivocally that these characteristics *can be* taught in school, when we set up pedagogies and curricula that foster deep, authentic learning, in which learners' full selves are engaged, and where social justice is of primary concern.

We need to germinate and grow the great leaders to come so that we can disrupt existing patterns of unequal access, systematic and implicit oppression and disparities in opportunities. With such entrenched inequality in our world, nourishing our children in the skills and virtues for social justice is of the utmost importance. We need to put decency and respect for self and others as highest priorities in our pedagogies. We must cultivate classrooms where thoughtful and equitable learning occurs, where all learners' full selves are engaged and where their immense potential as citizens is activated. We must begin this work by empowering young children.

References

Engel, S. (2021, June 19). Curiosity. *Slate School Education Idea Lab Virtual Summit.* https://ms-my.facebook.com/SlateSchool/videos/education-idea-lab-virtual-summit-presents-susan-engel/513046766713371/

Harris, E. A., & Alter, A. (2022, January 30). Book ban efforts spread across the U.S. *New York Times.* www.nytimes.com/2022/01/30/books/book-ban-us-schools.html

Kamenetz, A. (2022, February 1). More than half of teachers are looking for the exits, a poll says. *NPR*. www.npr.org/2022/02/01/1076943883/teachers-quitting-burnout

Louv, R. (2008). *Last child in the woods: Saving our children from nature-deficit disorder*. Algonquin Books.

McGee, E. O. (2021). *Black, brown, bruised: How racialized STEM education stifles innovation*. Harvard Education Press.

National Center for Education Statistics (n.d.). Public elementary/secondary school universe survey, 2001–02. Common Core of Data. http://nces.ed.gov/ccd/pubschuniv.asp

Sawchuk, S. (2021, June 11). What is critical race theory, and why is it under attack? *Education Week*. www.edweek.org/leadership/what-is-critical-race-theory-and-why-is-it-under-attack/2021/05

Sonu, D. (2020). Playing slavery in first grade: When "developmental appropriateness" goes awry in the progressive classroom. *Multicultural Perspectives*, *22*(2), 106–112. http://doi.org/10.1080/15210960.2020.1741369

Wong, J. C. (2021, May 25). The fight to whitewash US history: "A drop of poison is all you need." *The Guardian*. www.theguardian.com/world/2021/may/25/critical-race-theory-us-history-1619-project

World Almanac Education Group. (2006). *The world almanac and book of facts*. World Almanac Education Group.